Charities and Not-for-Profit Entities

Law and Practice

Available titles in this series include:

Agricultural Tenancies

Angela Sydenham

Change of Name

Nasreen Pearce

Child Care and Protection

Barbara Mitchels with Helen James

Debt Recovery in the Courts

John Kruse

Partnership and LLP Law

Elspeth Berry

Personal Injury Litigation

Gordon Exall

Procedure in Civil Courts and Tribunals

John Bowers QC and Eleena Misra

Residential Tenancies

Richard Colbey and Niamh O'Brien

Termination of Employment

John Bowers QC and Carol Davis

Wildy Practice Guides

Charities and Not-for-Profit Entities

Law and Practice

Cecile Gillard

Wildy, Simmonds and Hill Publishing

Gillard, Cecile

Charities and Not-for-Profit Entities, Law and Practice (Wildy Practice Guides series)

ISBN 9780854900749

Printed and bound in Great Britain

Contents

Preface

This book introduces legal practitioners to some of the most important features of charities and other not-for-profit entities, and alerts them to some of the key legal principles and regulatory requirements that affect those organisations. It can be used as a handy, quick reference, introductory guide by those whose legal specialisations lie elsewhere, but need to have a general understanding and basic outline knowledge of these wonderfully diverse, and heavily regulated, sectors.

Charities and not-for-profit organisations are part of what is increasingly termed 'civil society'. The alternative terms 'voluntary sector' and 'third sector' are still in common use to describe collectively the very wide range of non-commercial, social purpose organisations that exist in the UK. In the broadest context, all these terms can include organisations that are legally charities, as well as other not-for-profit organisations, such as members' clubs and societies, and even social enterprises (some of which are partially commercial organisations).

Company law applies across the UK. So, since the Companies Act 2006 came into force, companies registered in Northern Ireland are subject to both the primary and secondary UK company legislation. There is one combined companies register on which public details of all companies are displayed. An individual company is still registered in one of the constituent jurisdictions of the UK – England and Wales or Scotland or Northern Ireland – and it is not possible for a company to re-register in another jurisdiction (although it is, of course, free to operate in any of the jurisdictions).

There are important differences in the company law rules that affect 'old' companies (ie *incorporated prior to* 1 October 2009). This is because, as the phased implementation of the Companies Act 2006 occurred, the considerable body of secondary legislation enacted deliberately retained the impact of some parts of the old law and some provisions of existing companies' articles of association. In some cases the company's members can deliberately 'opt in' to the new, more liberal, rules by passing appropriate resolutions and/or altering their company's articles. Considerable care must therefore be taken in dealing with an old company to determine precisely which combination of legal rules and requirements apply to it.

References in this book to charitable companies are to companies limited by guarantee unless otherwise stated (there are very few companies limited by shares that are charities).

Charity law is a devolved matter so there are now separate statutes for each of the jurisdictions (Charities Act 2011 and surviving parts of the Charities Acts 1992 and 2006 for England and Wales, Charities and Trustee Investment (Scotland) Act 2005 for Scotland and the Charities Act (Northern Ireland) 2008 for Northern Ireland), together with separate supporting regulations. The principles and requirements affecting charities in each of those three jurisdictions are now substantially different. It is also likely that as case law and regulatory practice develop there will be further future divergence.

Each jurisdiction has (or, in the case of Northern Ireland, soon will have) a separate Register of Charities. There are differing levels of public information on each one and each charity regulator has its own systems and procedures for matters such as the charity registration number. In Scotland the register is all encompassing – any organisation that is a charity under the law of Scotland is on the register. This is still not the case in England and Wales for several reasons. There is a minimum income level for registration of charities (for further details, see Chapter 1). In addition, some 'exemptions' and 'exceptions' from registration remain and the English legislation does not require registration of charities established under the law of another jurisdiction.

The law in Scotland demands registration of any charitable organisation that is established under the law of another jurisdiction but is managed or controlled wholly or mainly in Scotland or has a significant presence in Scotland (for more details, see Chapter 1). This results in a registration requirement for many 'cross border' charities, in particular those established in England and Wales that operate in Scotland as well. Comments about some key aspects of charity law in Scotland are included in this book, which will assist those who may be affected by this dual regulation.

At the date of preparation of this book, the legislation enabling registration of Scottish Charitable Incorporated Organisations (SCIOs) has been brought into force and SCIOs can now be registered. However, the equivalent new legal forms in England and Wales and Northern Ireland are still awaited.

My thanks to the team at Wildy for their support as this book was being prepared. I am especially grateful to Andrew Riddoch for his kind encouragement, patience and expert guidance (and some good coffee and excellent pastries). Thanks are also due to many professional colleagues, past and present, from whom I have learnt a very great deal, particularly Peter Van Duzer, David Impey, Philip Kirkpatrick, Alice Faure Walker, Kirsty Semple, Greyham Dawes and Ed Marsh.

It is my immense privilege to serve a rainbow array of wonderful charities. My experiences in doing so have facilitated and informed the contents of this book in many ways. I am deeply indebted to them all.

Cecile Gillard
March 2012

1 The Essentials of Charities and Not-for-Profits

1.1 What is a 'charity'?

A 'charity' in the legal sense is an organisation that:

- has exclusively charitable purposes (no non-charitable element is permitted); and

- provides charitable benefit to the public at large (or an adequate section of the public).

This is true of charities established under the law of England and Wales and of those charities that are established under the law of Scotland or the law of Northern Ireland. However, the lists of *purposes* that can potentially be charitable in each of those jurisdictions differ (see paras 1.1.1, 1.1.4 and 1.1.5).

The listed purposes are those *capable* of being charitable, in the right set of circumstances. Not every organisation with a relevant purpose will in fact be a charity. In addition, the lists are not definitive. The law is flexible, so that the legal meaning of 'charity' can develop as needs alter, society and social conditions change and new means to provide charitable benefits evolve.

There is a fundamental difference between an organisation's *purposes* and its *activities* in pursuit of those purposes. For example, fundraising is an activity, whereas advancing public education about wildlife is a purpose. The wildlife education charity needs to have the power to raise funds, for obvious reasons, but fundraising is not itself the charitable purpose.

1.1.1 Charitable purposes – England and Wales (Charities Act 2011)

The list of potentially charitable purposes under the law of England and Wales is:

1. The prevention or relief of poverty.

2. The advancement of education.

3. The advancement of religion.

    Religion can include:

    • a religion which involves belief in more than one god; and

    • a religion which does not involve belief in a god.

4. The advancement of health or the saving of lives. This includes the prevention or relief of sickness, disease or human suffering.

5. The advancement of citizenship or community development. This can include rural or urban regeneration and the promotion of civic responsibility, volunteering, the voluntary sector or the effectiveness or efficiency of charities.

6. The advancement of the arts, culture, heritage or science.

7. The advancement of amateur sport. This can include sport or games which promote health by involving physical or mental skill or exertion.

8. The advancement of human rights, conflict resolution or reconciliation, the promotion of religious or racial harmony or equality and diversity.

9. The advancement of environmental protection or improvement.

10. The relief of those in need by reason of youth, age, ill-health, disability, financial hardship or other disadvantage. This can include relief given by the provision of accommodation or care to the relevant persons.

11. The advancement of animal welfare.

12. The promotion of the efficiency of the armed forces of the Crown, or of the efficiency of the police, fire and rescue services or ambulance services.

13. Any other purposes:

    (i)   that are not within 1–12 above but are recognised as charitable under section 5 of the 2011 Act (recreational and similar trusts) or under the old law;

    (ii) that are analogous to, or within the spirit of, 1–12 above;

    (iii) that may reasonably be regarded as analogous to, or within the spirit of, any purposes which have been recognised, under the law relating to charities in England and Wales, as falling within (ii) above or this sub-paragraph (iii).

This 'sweeper' category is important in carrying forward all existing charitable purposes not explicitly set out in the list. It also provides future flexibility so that the law can change and expand as society changes.

For the purposes of 13 above 'the old law' means law relating to charities in England and Wales in force immediately before 1 April 2008.

1.1.2   Recreational and similar trusts

Provision of facilities for recreation or leisure-time occupation, in the interests of social welfare, can be charitable, provided that these conditions are met (section 5 of the Charities Act 2011):

(a)   the facilities are provided with the object of improving the conditions of life for persons for whom the facilities are primarily intended; and

(b)   those persons have need of the facilities by reason of their youth, age, infirmity or disability, poverty or social and economic circumstances; or

(c)   the facilities are to be available to the public at large or to male or female members of the public.

The Act specifies that this applies in particular to village halls, community centres and women's institutes, as well to as the provision and maintenance of grounds and buildings for recreation or leisure-time occupation, always subject to the requirement that the facilities are provided in the interests of social welfare.

The usual charitable public benefit requirements also apply to such charitable purposes.

1.1.3   Community amateur sports clubs (registered sports clubs)

A 'registered sports club' is a club registered by HM Revenue & Customs as an amateur sports club (in accordance with Chapter 9 of Part 13 of the Corporation Tax Act 2010). Such a club that is established for charitable purposes is to be treated as 'not so established' and cannot be a charity (section 6 of the Charities Act 2011). This means a sports club cannot have both community amateur sports club (CASC) and charitable status.

1.1.4   Charitable purposes – Scotland (Charities and Trustee Investment (Scotland) Act 2005)

The list of potentially charitable purposes under the law of Scotland is:

1.   The prevention or relief of poverty.

2.   The advancement of education.

3.   The advancement of religion.

4.   The advancement of health. This can include the prevention or relief of sickness, disease or human suffering.

5.   The saving of lives.

6.   The advancement of citizenship or community development. This can include rural or urban regeneration and the promotion of civic responsibility, volunteering, the voluntary sector or the effectiveness or efficiency of charities.

7.   The advancement of the arts, heritage, culture or science.

8.   The advancement of public participation in sport (involving physical skill and exertion).

9.   The provision of recreational facilities, or organisation of recreational activities, with the object of improving the conditions of life for the persons for whom they are primarily intended. This applies only to recreational facilities or activities that are:

   •   primarily intended for persons who have need of them because of their age, ill-health, disability, financial hardship or other disadvantage; or

   •   available to members of the public at large or to male or female members of the public at large.

10.   The advancement of human rights, conflict resolution or reconciliation.

11.   The promotion of religious or racial harmony.

12.   The promotion of equality and diversity.

13.   The advancement of environmental protection or improvement.

14.   The relief of those in need by reason of age, ill-health, disability, financial hardship or other disadvantage. This can include relief given by the provision of accommodation or care.

15. The advancement of animal welfare.

16. Other purposes reasonably analogous to any of the purposes above.

The advancement of any philosophical belief (whether or not involving belief in a god) can be analogous to the purpose set out at 3 above.

1.1.5 Charitable purposes – Northern Ireland (Charities (Northern Ireland) Act 2008)

The list of potentially charitable purposes under the law of Northern Ireland is:

1. The prevention or relief of poverty.

2. The advancement of education.

3. The advancement of religion. 'Religion' includes:

   • a religion which involves belief in one god or more than one god; and

   • any analogous philosophical belief (whether or not involving belief in a god).

4. The advancement of health or the saving of lives. The advancement of health includes the prevention or relief of sickness, disease or human suffering.

5. The advancement of citizenship or community development. This includes rural or urban regeneration, and the promotion of civic responsibility, volunteering, the voluntary section or the effectiveness or efficiency of charities.

6. The advancement of the arts, culture, heritage or science.

7. The advancement of amateur sport, ie sports or games which promote health by involving physical or mental skill or exertion.

8. The advancement of human rights, conflict resolution or reconciliation, the promotion of religious or racial harmony or equality and diversity (this includes the advancement of peace and good community relations).

9. The advancement of environmental protection or improvement.

10. The relief of those in need by reason of youth, age, ill-health, disability, financial hardship or other disadvantage (this includes

relief given by the provision of accommodation or care to the persons mentioned).

11. The advancement of animal welfare.

12. Any other existing purposes, and analogous purposes.

1.1.6   The essential nature of charities

The essential nature of charities is to be organisations that exist for others. It is that characteristic which encourages people to make donations, to become trustees, to offer their time and talents as volunteers and perhaps also to leave legacies, so the good work can go on after they die.

1.1.7   Other key features of charities

Other key features of charities are that they:

- are subject to the ultimate supervision of the courts;

- are subject to day-to-day supervision by the relevant charity regulator;

- must meet the legal obligations for charities, particularly in relation to providing public benefit and observing restrictions on their activities and the use of their funds and assets;

- are publicly accountable to a range of interested parties;

- must be transparent and operate with integrity and honesty;

- must be independent of the state and, in general, independent of all others.

The requirement for independence means that trustees must govern and manage a charity solely in the overall interests of that charity, with consideration for the beneficiaries both present and future. It also means they must serve the charity alone – not the preferences of the charity's founder, or the interests of the person or body who appointed them, or even the interests of the charity's members, if it is a membership charity. Nor should the trustees act in accordance with the views or interests of funders, commercial partners or sponsors of the charity. Trustees must also disregard their own personal interests.

Charitable funds and assets must be applied properly. They are effectively held in custodianship by the trustees to be used only for the relevant charitable purposes. The charity must also use its powers to that end. The trustees must ensure the charity does all this.

Because charities are publicly accountable and transparent, a great deal of information about them is readily available in the public domain – who their trustees and their beneficiaries are; what their charitable purposes are; information about their current activities and future plans; details of their funds and assets, where those came from and how they are being used and so on.

1.2   Charity law and regulation

The activities of charities are regulated. Charity law imposes a wide range of obligations, controls and other requirements on charities and on their trustees. These have one clear and fundamental purpose – to protect charitable funds and assets and ensure they are correctly applied.

Charitable status carries responsibilities: the organisation in question must continue to pursue its stated charitable purposes and also continue to deliver suitable public benefit as it does that. The relevant charity regulator monitors the delivery of public benefit, to ensure it remains adequate. If the organisation fails to pursue its purposes and deliver suitable public benefit, and it cannot or will not make changes to address the situation, the charity regulator may intervene, appointing new trustees, giving directions and guidance, restructuring the charity and (rarely) removing it from the register of charities.

1.2.1   Charities Act 2011

A consolidating Act, the Charities Act 2011, is in force from March 2012. The Act repeals and replaces the Recreational Charities Act 1958, the Charities Act 1993 (as amended by the Charities Act 2006) and many, but not all, of the provisions of the Charities Act 2006. It does not make any substantive changes to the law.

Practitioners should note that:

•   regulations supplement the principal Act; and

•   some provisions of the Charities Act 1992 remain in force, in particular the provisions regarding professional fundraisers and commercial participators.

Built into the 2006 legislation was a requirement for a review after 5 years and that separate exercise began in Autumn 2011. The aims are to report on the operation and effectiveness of the legislation (now in the 2011 Act) and to consider whether further changes could be made to improve the legal and regulatory framework for charities. A report to the Minister for the Cabinet Office is expected to be laid before Parliament prior to the summer 2012 recess, however any subsequent Bill for further reform is not likely until 2015 or later.

1.2.2   The role of the courts

All charities are subject to the ultimate supervision of the courts – the High Court in England and Wales, the Court of Session in Scotland and the High Court in Northern Ireland. The powers of the courts are directed to the protection of charitable assets and to ensuring those assets are properly applied for the particular charitable purposes for which they have been given or otherwise provided. The day-to-day regulatory supervision of charities is undertaken by the three UK charity regulators.

1.2.3   First Tier Tribunal (Charities) – England and Wales

The First Tier Tribunal (Charity) (formerly called the Charity Tribunal) can:

- hear appeals against the decisions of the Charity Commission;
- hear applications for review of decisions of the Charity Commission;
- consider references from the Attorney General or the Charity Commission on points of law.

The Tribunal only has jurisdiction in respect of certain Charity Commission decisions made on or after 18 March 2008. These are specified in Schedule 6 to the Charities Act 2011. An appeal can only be made to the Tribunal by a charity after that charity has used the Commission's own decision review process and a final decision has been issued on the matter in question by the Commission.

1.2.4   Charity Commission

The Charity Commission is the regulator of charities in England and Wales. A corporate body, its legal authority flows from the Charities Act 2011 which gives it statutory objectives, functions, duties and powers.

The Commission's statutory functions are:

1. To determine whether or not institutions are charities.

2. To encourage and facilitate the better administration of charities.

3. To identify and investigate the apparent misconduct or mismanagement in the administration of charities, and take remedial or protective action in connection with misconduct or mismanagement.

4.   To determine whether public collection certificates should be issued and remain in force.

5.   To obtain, evaluate and disseminate information in connection with the performance of the Commission's functions or the meeting of its objectives.

6.   To give information or advice, or make proposals, to Ministers on matters relating to the Commission's functions or objectives.

So, the Commission is responsible for keeping the public Register of Charities in England and Wales and also deals with new charity registrations. It issues guidance on many areas, such as financial controls and trustees' responsibilities. It also issues guidance on the public benefit requirements for charities and monitors whether or not existing charities continue to have charitable purposes in law and are delivering suitable public benefit. The Commission also ensures charities meet their public reporting and accounting obligations.

1.2.5   Charity law and regulation in Scotland and in Northern Ireland

The regulator for charities in Scotland is the Office of the Scottish Charity Regulator (the OSCR) and the principal legislation is the Charities and Trustee Investment (Scotland) Act 2005. There is an independent Scottish Charity Appeals Panel to which appeals against decisions of the OSCR can be made.

The regulator for Northern Ireland is the Charity Commission for Northern Ireland and the principal legislation is the Charities (Northern Ireland) Act 2008, which is being brought into force in stages (with main implementation planned for 2012/13).

1.3   Charity registration

A charity with annual income of £5,000 or more must register with the Charity Commission. Far fewer charities are now 'exempt' or 'excepted' from this because of reforms originally introduced by the Charities Act 2006. The larger charities affected by those changes (annual income over £100,000) were registered first by the Charity Commission under a staged programme.

Charity law in Scotland takes a different approach, obliging all charitable organisations to register, regardless of size.

In both cases, the register of charities is publicly accessible on the regulators' websites:

- Charity Commission, www.charitycommission.gov.uk;

- OSCR, www.oscr.org.uk.

The registration of charities in Northern Ireland is being implemented in stages (from 2012/13).

1.4   Social enterprises

The term 'social enterprise' does not have a specific legal meaning, unlike 'charity' and 'charitable purposes'.

A social enterprise is an organisation that undertakes some form of trading or business activity, aiming to operate sustainably over the longer term. What marks it out from a commercial enterprise is its overriding purpose – that will be a social objective (rather than purely commercial profit maximisation for the benefit of its owners). Because of this, a social enterprise applies most and sometimes all of its surplus profits by reinvesting them in its social-purpose activities or investing them in the wider community.

Social enterprises can take a range of different legal forms, including industrial and provident societies, private companies limited by guarantee or shares and community interest companies (CICs).

1.4.1   Community interest companies

CICs are a special optional corporate legal form for social and community enterprise activities. A CIC is a type of company, subject to general company law and also to CIC-specific requirements and regulations (see the Companies (Audit, Investigations and Community Enterprise) Act 2004 as amended by the Companies Act 2006 (Commencement No 2, Consequential Amendments, Transitional Provisions and Savings) Order 2007 (SI 2007/1093) and the Community Interest Company Regulations 2005 (SI 2005/1788) (as amended by the Community Interest Company (Amendment) Regulations 2009 (SI 2009/1942)).

A CIC has independent legal identity, separate from its members and directors. It is capable of holding assets, entering into contracts and other legal arrangements, employing staff and enforcing its own legal rights.

The members of a CIC have the protection of limited liability. This operates through the usual company law mechanisms because a CIC is either a public or private company limited by shares or a private company limited by guarantee. However, the CIC itself is entirely liable for its own debts (and can become insolvent). Other legal entities can enforce any legal rights and claims they have against a CIC.

Registration of a CIC requires a paper-based application to the Regulator of Community Interest Companies (CIC Regulator). If the CIC Regulator approves the application it is then passed to Companies House for registration of the new CIC. There are two fees payable on registration – one to the CIC Regulator and another to Companies House.

Because CICs must be established for community benefit purposes, there are a range of significant legal restrictions on how their funds and assets can be used. There are also controls on how CICs can be funded. These affect how a CIC can raise funds, for example by limiting the amounts it can pay on dividend bearing shares. There are also controls on what payments a CIC can make to its directors and public disclosure requirements regarding directors' remuneration and benefits.

On winding up, the final surplus funds of a CIC can only be applied in certain ways. The destination of those funds partly depends upon the constitution of the CIC as well as upon the relevant legislative provisions. In some cases the CIC Regulator will determine to which entities the funds are to be transferred.

1.4.2   The community interest test

Every CIC must deliver benefit to the community – it must meet the 'community interest test'. The 'community' in this context can be the entire community or a definable sector or group, sharing a common characteristic, which a reasonable person might regard as a section of the community.

The 'benefit' is assessed by reference to what a reasonable person might consider to be a benefit to the community in question. In order to become a CIC an entity must satisfy the CIC Regulator that it will deliver such benefit and it must do this before it can be incorporated by the Registrar of Companies at Companies House (or re-registered as a CIC from some other legal form).

The CIC must continue to meet this test on an ongoing basis. Compliance is monitored by the CIC Regulator.

1.4.3 Regulation and accountability

CICs are dual regulated. The CIC Regulator supervises them in relation to CIC-specific legal requirements and the Registrar of Companies does so in relation to company filing requirements. The CIC Regulator has a significant range of powers to ensure the adequate and effective supervision of CICs.

CICs are subject to wider public accountability and reporting requirements than private companies. Every year a CIC must file a 'community interest company report' with its annual accounts and reports. That is monitored by the CIC Regulator to ensure the community interest test is still being met.

1.5 Other not-for-profits

'Not-for-profits' describes a wide and varied range of organisations. It encompasses sports and social clubs, associations, professional bodies, scientific and medical institutions and many others. A not-for-profit organisation can be in many different legal forms, though the most common are unincorporated members' associations and companies (usually limited by guarantee).

1.6 Typical legal forms for charities and not-for-profits

Charities, social enterprises and other not-for-profits come in a wide variety of legal forms. Some forms are specific to a particular range of activities, for example CICs are designed as vehicles for social enterprise and the charitable incorporated organisation (CIO) and its Scottish equivalent, the Scottish charitable incorporated organisation (SCIO) are only for charities. Other forms, such as unincorporated members' organisations or companies, are available to all.

The three most common legal forms used by charities (prior to the introduction of the CIO/SCIO) are:

- unincorporated charitable trust;
- unincorporated members' association;
- company limited by guarantee.

1.6.1 Key features of the most common legal forms

Unincorporated trust

Under the law of England and Wales, a trust has no independent legal identity. It has no formal legal membership, there are simply trustees. Those trustees do not have limited liability protection. A trust is often used for a grant-making charity that has no other activities of its own and is a relatively low risk operation. A charitable trust is subject to the general principles of trust law but above all it is subject to charity law.

Unincorporated members' association

An unincorporated members' association is a group of individuals associating together for a common purpose. It has no independent legal identity, which gives rise to legal and practical difficulties in holding and dealing with assets and entering into legal arrangements. There is a membership and also a group of trustees (usually the trustees are drawn from amongst a wider membership). Neither the trustees nor the members are protected by limited liability.

An unincorporated members' association is heavily dependent on its own constitution. The law regulating such associations is largely common law and has been little developed by statute. As stated above, one of the most important legal issues is that such organisations are not afforded their own distinct legal identity. This gives rise to a number of difficulties, including:

- The association cannot enter into contracts or other legal agreements in its own capacity – the officers must do so in their personal capacities (with attendant personal liabilities).

- The association cannot be held liable for wrongful acts committed by its representatives whilst acting on its behalf. This gives rise to personal liability risks for the individuals in question. Worse, it remains unclear the extent to which liability can extend to all the officers or even the general membership of the association – especially if the association's assets are insufficient to meet relevant liabilities to a third party.

- A member cannot sue for damages for injury sustained as a consequence of the wrongful act of an officer or fellow member acting on the association's behalf.

- The association cannot own property, so individual members or officers must hold the title in a trustee capacity. Title transfers are therefore necessary when personnel change.

Company limited by guarantee

A charitable company has its own independent legal identity. So it can have and enforce legal rights and is responsible for its own legal commitments and its own debts and liabilities. It has trustees (who are also directors for company law purposes) and it must also have members. There can be complete or partial commonality between the board and the membership or no overlap (subject to the terms of the charity's articles). Members and trustees are protected by limited liability under normal circumstances. Company law provides a clear legal framework for a charitable company (Companies Act 2006 and associated regulations), alongside charity law.

Other legal forms

Whilst not as common, other legal forms that are sometimes taken by some charities and not-for-profits include:

- *Royal Charter bodies* – these are organisations of national standing and significant criteria would need to be satisfied before a charter could be sought (for instance, a national membership of at least 5,000).

- *Bodies established by specific statutes* – this is particularly relevant to some National Health Service-related charities and some other specialist charities such as the National Trust.

- *Industrial and provident societies* – a significant number of social welfare housing organisations are in this legal form. Reform of industrial and provident law has only been partially achieved and a rather clumsy, inflexible and dated legal and regulatory framework still applies, somewhat unhappily requiring oversight of the Mutuals Register by the Financial Services Authority. These factors make this form unattractive for new ventures.

Tax

The tax implications of the choice of legal form, as well as the tax treatment of particular activities, should be considered. Tax may be chargeable on some or all of the organisation's income and gains (ie it may be subject to direct taxation).

There is no general exemption for tax for charities. However, charities have a very wide range of highly beneficial charity specific tax exemptions. A particular exemption will only be available if the applicable rules and conditions for it are met.

Of particular importance is the tax exemption for income generated by 'primary purpose trading', ie trading in *direct* pursuit of the charity's charitable purposes. Examples of primary purpose trading are:

- an arts charity that operates a theatre in order to educate the public in the performing arts selling tickets to artistic performances;
- an educational charity that sells appropriate educational publications and resources;
- a charity that cares for a heritage building charging for admission to the premises.

Ancillary trading related to the primary purpose can also be tax exempt, for instance the theatre selling programmes and refreshments to its audiences.

There are no limits to the amount of primary purpose trading that can be carried out tax free. However, the charity's trustees must be mindful of the public benefit requirements and ensure that any fees charged do not unduly restrict access to the charity's services and facilities. The Charity Commission guidance *Public Benefit and Fee Charging* (see www.charitycommission.gov.uk) should be considered carefully in this respect.

Other tax exemptions of particular importance include those which facilitate tax free giving to charities by individuals and companies, such as the Gift Aid scheme.

In general, there are no tax exemptions or special tax advantages for non-charitable not-for-profit entities. However, CASCs are able to receive Gift Aid donations. CICs do not have any special tax exemptions or advantages.

VAT is a tax on transactions that occur when goods or services are supplied during business activities (other than 'exempt supplies' goods or services). It must be charged by suppliers if their turnover is above the VAT registration threshold. The VAT requirements apply regardless of the legal form of an organisation involved in a relevant transaction and regardless of whether that organisation is motivated by profit.

Note that 'business activities' has a complex and wide meaning in the context of this indirect tax. So, for VAT purposes, charities and not-for-profits can be involved in 'business activities' and therefore must pay VAT on goods and services they buy or, subject to relevant VAT registration thresholds, charge it on goods and services they provide to others. A 'taxable supply' of goods or services for VAT purposes will incur the applicable VAT rate for the type of supply – standard or reduced or zero rate.

There are only a few, very limited, exemptions from VAT available to charities. The VAT rules are designed for commercial businesses, so they do not 'fit' easily with organisations operating in a non-commercial way. Many such organisations find they have significant irrecoverable VAT – prior to the increase in the standard rate of VAT, it was estimated that the charity sector alone was losing at least £1 billion in irrecoverable VAT every year. An additional £145 million has been added to that figure by the 20% standard rate.

Taxation is a highly complex area. It poses particular risks and problems for charities and not-for-profits, especially in the context of VAT. Specialist tax advice should always be taken by such organisations.

Accounting and reporting

All organisations need to keep day-to-day accounting records in order to manage their affairs properly and keep track of their assets and liabilities. What legal requirements apply to those records, and whether or not the organisation is obliged to prepare and file public annual accounts, will depend on the legal type of the organisation.

Registered charities in England and Wales must prepare and file public annual accounts and an annual trustees' report with the Charity Commission. There are exemptions for the smallest charities. All charities on the Scottish Register have public accounting obligations, regardless of their income level. Accounting obligations will also apply to charities in Northern Ireland, where there will be new regulations made under the Charities Act (Northern Ireland) 2008. The new obligations are expected to take effect in 2012/13.

All companies, including charities, must file public annual accounts at Companies House within 9 months of their financial year end. This applies to CICs, which must include additional disclosures and information in their accounts and also provide a 'community interest' report.

For further details about these public accountability requirements, see Chapter 5.

2 Governance and Management

2.1 What governance is

Organisations need to be governed by a group of individuals who collectively form the governing body and together govern that organisation. Governance is how the organisation is operated and controlled by those who have responsibility for the ultimate management of that organisation. There is no formal legal definition of 'governance' specific to charities and not-for-profit bodies.

In the corporate commercial sector the original description often used for governance was:

> The systems and processes concerned with ensuring the overall direction, effectiveness and accountability of an organisation.

The key aspects of governance which that description identifies are:

- giving direction;
- enhancing effectiveness; and
- ensuring accountability.

The chosen methods (systems and processes) of governance are directed towards these key aspects.

Governance is now often described as 'adding long-term value' to the organisation. In the context of charities and not-for-profit organisations, the 'value' is generally improving the level and quality of benefits delivered to the beneficiaries or the wider community and ensuring the long-term viability and effectiveness of the entity, rather than enhancing financial value for current and future shareholders or other investors.

2.1.1 The appropriate means to the right end

Governance is not an end in itself. Rather it is a *means* towards the twin *ends* of:

- good strategic management of the whole organisation; and

- practical risk management, appropriate to the activities and proportionate to the circumstances.

The governing body is responsible for the well-being of the entire organisation. This has a collective dimension – the board or committee acting together in the proper governance of the entity – and an individual one – each board member having his or her own responsibility to play an active part in that.

2.2   What governance is not

Governance is not the same as the day-to-day management of the organisation or its practical operation (eg the carrying out of activities or the provision of services to the public or specific beneficiaries), nor is it routine internal administration. Governance is at a higher, strategic level. It is about creating the vision and setting the strategy and the policies that facilitate the pursuit of that vision and the achievement of that strategy.

Individuals serving on the board of a charity or other not-for-profit are often deeply motivated by particular areas of personal interest and commitment (for instance, the organisation's educational work). This can generate valuable energy and enthusiasm but may risk narrowing their focus. It is important for the governing body as a whole and the individuals who serve on it to see the 'bigger picture' and address their efforts to the whole organisation.

2.3   Who is responsible for governance?

The governing body is responsible for governance in the organisation. In practice, this is often not as straightforward as that statement might suggest. Often, the name of the governing body does not immediately suggest its formal legal role. Another common practical issue is identifying which body is *the* governing body, especially if the entity has a number of different committees, operating with little or no coordination. This can create a lack of clarity as to the overall structure and uncertainty about where the strategic leadership and highest level decision-making actually rests.

In addition, many not-for-profits are entirely volunteer led and operated, so people have multiple roles and those who sit on the governing body may also be active volunteers, delivering the services or carrying out the activities. If the organisation has a membership structure, some or all of the board will probably also be members. Lay volunteers, without any legal knowledge and experience, are unlikely to make clear distinctions between which 'hat' they wear at any given time. So, their strategic management role, as members of the governing body, is rarely clearly distinguished in their minds from their separate roles as 'sharp end' volunteers. Their actions often confuse their capacities, and the organisation's documents and records are frequently muddled, unclear, inadequate or even legally incorrect in demonstrating who did or decided what in which capacity. This carries serious legal risks.

2.4 Governance in context for civil society organisations

The transparency and accountability of civil society organisations should reflect the very essence of the civil society sector – selflessness and public service. Whilst following good governance processes is certainly important, common sense, honesty and personal integrity are of paramount importance in managing any body that exists for the benefit of wider society and/or is entrusted with public funding or donations from the general public.

The main objective of governance in the civil society sector should therefore be improving effectiveness in order to enhance the positive social impact of the organisation, whilst safeguarding its long-term future. Governance should help decision-making and assist the work of the board, supporting the efforts of those who voluntarily and generously give their time and talents as leaders of and volunteers for charities and not-for-profit bodies.

2.4.1 Governance standards and tools for the civil society sector

The Hallmarks of an Effective Charity (CC10) sets out what the Charity Commission regards as the key principles of good governance for charities, with examples of how to put these into practice. It is a good starting point for civil society sector governance standards in general and can be downloaded from the Commission's website (see www.charitycommission.gov.uk).

Good Governance: A Code for the Voluntary and Community Sector (2nd edn, October 2010) (the Code) (see www.charitycommission.gov.uk) provides a framework that can be adapted to specific organisations' needs and circumstances. The Code has been developed by representatives of key sector bodies, with support from the Charity Commission.

The Code uses six high level principles it suggests are universally applicable to good governance and leadership in voluntary and community organisations:

- understanding the board's role;

- delivery of organisational purpose;

- working effectively (individually and collectively);

- exercising effective control;

- behaving with integrity; and

- being open and accountable.

Codes and standards designed for the commercial sector can also be used as reference points. However, it can be difficult to adapt such material for application to a non-commercial body without some prior knowledge and experience in both governance of voluntary bodies and the special needs and circumstances of the civil society sector. In addition, models developed for the commercial sector concern themselves with issues that are not relevant to voluntary organisations (such as shareholder-related issues). They are also written for a larger size of organisation and greater scale of operations than are likely to be found in a typical charity or not-for-profit.

The checklist below provides some reference points for use in tailoring a governance regime that meets the needs of the particular organisation – one size certainly does not fit all.

2.4.2   Checklist – sources of further information and reference: civil society sector governance

Charities Evaluation Services

Charities Evaluation Services (CES) is a charity established to increase the effectiveness of the voluntary sector by developing its use of evaluation and quality systems (www.ces-vol.org.uk).

Charity regulators

The charity regulators provide general guidance for trustees about their role and responsibilities, as well as guidance on complying with specific legal requirements for public accountability (including accounting and reporting obligations and applicable time limits for filing necessary items):

- Charity Commission, www.charitycommission.gov.uk;

- OSCR, www.oscr.org.uk;

- Charity Commission for Northern Ireland, www.charitycommissionni.org.uk.

Note the regulators cannot provide specific legal, accounting or tax advice to trustees. Suitable professional advisers, with experience in the context of charities, should be consulted for such advice.

Directory of Social Change

The Directory of Social Change (DSC) promotes positive social change and provides a wide range of reference and training resources and activities (www.dsc.org.uk).

Institute of Chartered Secretaries and Administrators

The Institute of Chartered Secretaries and Administrators (ICSA) issues guidance notes as well as providing training events and publications of relevance to the charity sector and the wider voluntary sector. Its Charity Secretaries Group raises standards by promoting best practice. Group events increase skills and knowledge and enable people to develop their full potential (www.icsa.org.uk).

National Association for Voluntary and Community Action

The National Association for Voluntary and Community Action (NAVCA) is the national voice of local third sector groups and community services organisations (www.navca.org.uk).

National Council for Voluntary Organisations

The National Council for Voluntary Organisations (NCVO) provides a range of information and advice on governance and trusteeship (www.ncvo-vol.org.uk/governanceandleadership).

Scottish Council for Voluntary Organisations

The Scottish Council for Voluntary Organisations (SCVO) supports voluntary sector organisations in Scotland with a range of information, resources, training and other services (www.scvo.org.uk).

Small Charities Coal rustee Network

The Small Charities coalition (now amalgamated with the Charity Trustee Network (CTN)) helps trustees share experience and knowledge. It also signposts further information and sources of help (www.smallcharities.org.uk).

Wales Council for Voluntary Action

The Wales Council for Voluntary Action (WCVA) represents the interests of voluntary organisations in Wales. Its activities include training services and reference materials relating to trustees and governance matters (www.wcva.org.uk).

2.4.3 Application of the general law to charities and other not-for-profits

Members of governing bodies need to understand that their organisation operates subject to the wider law and to take suitable professional advice on all relevant areas (such as health and safety, insurance, employment law, tax and VAT). Breaches of such wider legal requirements may result in penalties against the organisation and sometimes against the members of its governing body.

It is essential that appropriate risk management procedures are in place and actually followed in practice. Appropriate insurance cover should be arranged and regularly reviewed, though boards should recognise that insurance is no substitute for appropriate management of risks.

Important distinctions must be drawn between insurance that benefits the organisation, for example in relation to loss or damage to its assets or insurance in relation to its potential liabilities, and insurance intended to benefit the individual members of the governing body. There are particular legal issues in the context of insurance for trustees' personal liabilities being paid for out of the charity's funds. The limitations of any insurance cover also need to be clearly understood.

It is important to keep the right balance between making trustees and others aware of their responsibilities and being honest about the potential liabilities, without discouraging talented and good hearted individuals from giving valuable public service in the civil society sector. The reality is that any sensible person, paying attention to their organisation and its affairs and exercising a common sense approach, will be a valuable member of the governing body, and find great personal satisfaction in giving that service. Potential liabilities only become reality when things are very badly mismanaged or there are serious legal misunderstandings and mistakes. Such situations are fortunately a rarity.

2.5 Charities – the role of trustees

This is how the Charity Commission describes the trustees' role (*The Essential Trustee: What you need to know* (CC3) (see www.charitycommission.gov.uk)):

> Trustees have and must accept ultimate responsibility for directing the affairs of a charity, and ensuring that it is solvent, well-run, and delivering the charitable outcomes for the benefit of the public for which it has been set up.

The OSCR states in its *Guidance for Charity Trustees*, '*acting with care and diligence*' (see www.oscr.org.uk):

> Charity trustees ... are collectively ... responsible for all the activities of the charity ... They have a collective duty of care for the charity ... Charity trustees are expected to act together as a board ... to realise the values and purposes of the charity ...

In summary, the trustees:

- are responsible for governance;
- bear ultimate responsibility for the charity;
- must give direction to the organisation;
- must be in control of the charity and its affairs;
- must ensure the charity pursues its own charitable purposes and delivers the public benefit for which it is established;
- must ensure the charity operates within its own constitution; and
- must ensure the charity acts lawfully and deals with its specific legal obligations.

Trustees of charities need to balance the interests of both current and potential future beneficiaries, ensuring the longer-term viability of the organisation. Trustees must also govern the charity independently, regardless of their own personal interests or those of their family members or any other organisation or body to which they or their families are connected. Conflicts of interest need to be identified and dealt with. Particular issues arise where a third party exercises direct appointment rights to place an individual on the board.

The law sets particular legal responsibilities for trustees because they have custody of the funds and assets entrusted to the charity for its particular charitable purposes. Those purposes are aimed at providing appropriate public benefit (to a specific beneficiary group or the public at large), hence the need for legal safeguards and wide public accountability. It is in this context that trustees should understand that they are stewards on behalf of others.

Professional advisers have an important role to play in ensuring trustees are aware of their role. This is not least because, despite all the publicity and public comment over charity law changes in the various jurisdictions of the UK, some charity trustees still fail to recognise the legal responsibilities of the position they hold.

2.5.1   The legal position of charity trustees

Charity trustees are the people having the general control of the management and administration of the charity (section 177 of the Charities Act 2011, section 106 of the Charities and Trustee Investment (Scotland) Act 2005). There is an overriding legal requirement that charity trustees act in the best interests of the charity, ensuring it pursues its charitable purposes and delivers adequate public benefit.

2.5.2   Trustees' duties – England and Wales

Charity law in England and Wales imposes duties on trustees because they hold a position of utmost trust, which must be discharged with honesty and integrity. The more general duties, such as the overriding duty to act in the best interests of the charity, are largely common law duties. Specific duties also exist, usually because of particular provisions in English charity legislation, especially the Charities Act 2011, the Trustee Act 2000 (which has particular relevance to the trustees of unincorporated charities) and the many sets of related regulations.

The trustees of CIOs will have some specific duties, including a duty to further the CIO's purposes (this also applies as a duty of the CIO's members). If a CIO trustee has particular special knowledge or experience, or acts as a trustee in the course of a business or profession, that trustee is subject to higher standards in the performance of his or her general trustee duties (section 221(2) of the Charities Act 2011).

2.5.3   Trustees' duties – Scotland

Charity law in Scotland imposes both specific duties on charity trustees (eg in relation to investments) and general duties. The general duties set the context in which trustees must govern and manage their charities.

Those general duties of charity trustees are specified in the legislation (unlike the position in England and Wales). They are:

- To act in the best interests of the charity.

- To ensure the charity acts consistently with its purposes (ie its charitable purposes or 'objects').

- To act with the care and diligence it is reasonable to expect of someone managing the affairs of another person.

- To ensure the charity complies with the requirements of the Charities and Trustee Investment (Scotland) Act 2005 and other legislation.

The trustees of any charity on the Scottish Charity Register must comply with these duties. The law specifically provides that any breach of them is to be treated as misconduct in the administration of the charity (section 66(4) of the Charities and Trustee Investment (Scotland) Act 2005). So, at least in theory, the OSCR can take regulatory action if a charity's trustees are in breach of their general duties.

2.5.4 Trustees' duties – the regulators' approach

Charity regulators take particular interest in certain areas (and, in many cases, have specific legal responsibilities to monitor and take preventative or remedial action when charitable assets appear to be at risk) and will also take particular interest in the conduct of the trustees in relation to those areas. The regulators have considerable enforcement and protective powers available to them if the trustees are not conducting the charity's affairs adequately.

The key areas of greatest interest to the charity regulators are:

- the safeguarding and correct application of charitable funds and other assets;

- the active pursuit of the charity's charitable purposes and the delivery of adequate public benefit to the correct beneficiary group;

- full and timely compliance by charities with their public accounting and reporting obligations;

- avoidance of harmful conflicts of interest;

- avoidance of improper private benefits, including improper benefits to trustees and persons connected to trustees;

- compliance with the charity's constitution.

There is some truth in the adage 'regulators follow the money' not least because charity law focuses on protecting charitable assets and ensuring they are applied to the charitable purposes for which they were given. If all of that is under control and the charity's public reporting is good, the trustees will find the regulators take a fairly benign and supportive role.

2.5.5 Charity trustees and conflicts of interest – general

Trustees must always act in the charity's best interests and must not allow their judgment to be clouded by personal interests. Any potentially conflicting personal interest which is material in nature ought to be declared to the whole trustee body so that:

- the board is aware of it;

- any potential conflict of interest (ie between the charity's interests and the trustee's personal interests) can be identified and eliminated or managed;

- any constitutional bar on interested trustees can be observed (eg an interested trustee may be prevented from attending/counting in the quorum and/or voting at the relevant trustees' meeting(s));

- any potential harm to the charity arising from a conflict can be prevented;

- the trustees can be seen to be acting 'with clean hands' and the charity's governance can be seen to be independent and effective.

Potentially conflicting interests include financial and other material interests and also extend to the interests of family members (eg spouses, civil partners and children) or other bodies to which a trustee is connected (the trustee's employer or his own business, the company in which a trustee holds shares, the local authority which the trustee serves as a councillor or officer, a body that directly appointed the trustee, etc). Boards and their members should also be aware of the potential for substantial conflicts of *loyalty* arising.

It is good practice to maintain a register of trustees' personal interests and to update it periodically and also whenever a trustee notifies a new or altered interest. All new trustees should be asked to declare any relevant potentially conflicting interests to the charity (or state they are not aware of any). It is best practice to use a written declaration and to keep that document in the charity's records. An annual circulation to all trustees, reminding them to declare any changes in their interests, is also advisable, since personal circumstances and personal connections to individuals and organisations can and will change over time.

Where a particular agenda item at a board meeting may relate to a trustee's potentially conflicting interests, the chairman should address the matter at the commencement of the meeting, before any discussion on that item occurs or any decision is taken on it. The chairman may also choose to remind trustees generally of their duties to declare potentially conflicting interests from time to time. Some opt to do so at the start of each board meeting.

2.5.6 Conflicts of interest – directly appointed charity trustees

Particular care is needed when a trustee has been directly appointed by a body or organisation that has appointment powers under the charity's constitution. The immediate and general issue is that of maintaining independence and fulfilling the general duties of a trustee.

The trustee does not act as the nominee or representative of the appointing body. Rather, he or she must concentrate on the interests of the charity and on ensuring it delivers adequate public benefit to its beneficiaries, regardless of the interests of the appointing body. It is important that the appointing body understands this and vital that the individual trustee does.

Where a particular body has exercised such direct appointment rights to place a trustee on a charity's board, subsequent specific conflicts of interest may arise. Examples include where the appointor is being approached as a potential funder or where the charity is negotiating to enter service provision contracts or other legal arrangements with the appointor. Such specific conflicts must be identified and dealt with correctly and transparently.

Charity law in Scotland (section 66(1)(c) of the Charities and Trustee Investment (Scotland) Act 2005) specifically provides that, in situations where there is a conflict of interest between the charity and the person responsible for a trustee's appointment, that trustee must:

• put the interests of the charity before that other person;

• where any other duty prevents him or her doing so, disclose the conflicting interest to the charity and refrain from participating in any deliberation or decision of the trustees on the matter in question.

Whilst there is no directly comparable provision in the Charities Act 2011, trustees of charities in England and Wales would be well advised to follow this pattern of behaviour in such circumstances.

2.5.7   Trustee remuneration, benefits and personal interests

Trusteeship is an essentially selfless position. As the Charity Commission has rightly commented:

> The principle of voluntary trusteeship remains central to the ethos of the charity sector.

So, the law still regards charity trusteeship as a voluntary role and generally requires trustees to act without remuneration or other form of material personal benefit. In addition, as has been illustrated above, the duties of trustees and the very essence of their role is that they act on behalf of others, for the greater good of society in general, regardless of their personal interests.

The meaning of 'benefit' in this context is very wide. It covers direct and indirect payments, all kinds of financial benefits, benefits in kind (such as free or reduced cost accommodation in property owned by the charity), commercial benefits under a contract or other legal agreement or arrangement, employment of a trustee, payments for being a trustee, payments for providing services to the charity other than as a trustee and 'honoraria'.

This general principle that trustees may not take personal private benefit from their charity extends to benefits for people and organisations to which a trustee is connected – for example, family members or corporate bodies or other businesses in which the trustee or the trustee's family members have interests.

It is as a result of this important principle that charity constitutions usually contain detailed and wide prohibitions on benefits of any kind to trustees. Such prohibitions must be strictly obeyed.

The general prohibition on private benefits is subject to some detailed but limited statutory exceptions under the relevant charity legislation in England and Wales and in Scotland. A broad outline of both is set out below. Similar exceptions are to apply in Northern Ireland when its new charity law takes effect.

It should be noted that:

- The legal systems in England and Wales and in Scotland do not have precisely the same rules, nor do exactly the same conditions apply to the two separate exceptions to the general 'no benefits' rule.

- If the organisation is in the legal form of a company, the company law rules on conflicts of interest and declarations/disclosures of interests must also be considered and observed.

This is a complex and potentially dangerous area, for charities and for trustees. Trustees would be very unwise to proceed with proposed transactions or arrangements that involve benefits to trustees and connected persons without taking independent professional advice

2.5.8 Trustee remuneration/transactions – sections 185–188 of the Charities Act 2011

The general rule remains that trustees must not benefit personally from their charity – the relevant Charities Act 2011 rules that permit the possibility of remuneration of trustees and connected persons *for services* do not permit remuneration of a trustee for holding the office of trustee. Further, any prohibition in the charity's own constitution on remuneration of trustees and connected persons must be obeyed – the Charities Act 2011 permissive provisions do not override such a prohibition.

The rules in the Charities Act 2011 apply to trustees and to 'connected persons'. These are trustees' spouses or civil partners, their parents, grandparents, children, grandchildren, brothers or sisters and the spouses or civil partners of any of those categories, and also to business partners of any of those categories and to any institution or corporate body controlled by those categories or such a business. 'Child' includes an adopted child, a stepchild and an illegitimate child.

The conditions imposed by the Act in relation to proposed remuneration for services are (in summary):

1. There must be *no* prohibition in the charity's constitution. (Note there *will* be such a provision in most constitutions of charities established prior to the implementation of the statutory permissive regime.)

2. The trustees must consider the proposed arrangements to be in the charity's best interests. (Note they must consider that the services in question are needed *and* that the trustee (or connected person) is the appropriate provider of those services.)

3. There must be a written agreement between the charity and the relevant person. This must contain particular provisions, including the maximum amount of the remuneration, which must be reasonable in the circumstances.

4. Less than half the trustees are to be subject to any such agreement at any time.

5. Before entering into any such agreement, the trustees must have taken into account Charity Commission guidance relating to such agreements.

The conflicted trustee (whether directly interested or indirectly, eg in a proposed arrangement that involves a 'connected person') is disqualified from acting in relation to any decision or any other matter connected with such a proposed agreement (section 186(2) of the Charities Act 2011).

The trustees are subject to their general duties when considering any possible use by the charity of these statutory provisions. The legislation also specifically imposes the statutory duty of skill and care in section 1(1) of the Trustee Act 2000 on the trustees when making decisions about such proposed arrangements. This applies regardless of the charity's legal form, so the trustees of charitable companies and other incorporated forms of charity are subject to it, in just the same way that trustees of unincorporated charities are.

The Charities Act 2011 provides this limited statutory exception to the 'no benefits' rule, to allow the *possibility* of remuneration for services other than services as a trustee. Even if the statutory conditions, outlined above, are met the trustees should think long and hard about whether it is actually right to make use of a trustee or connected person for the provision of the services. There are difficult issues in relation to controlling conflicts of interest and in retaining the clarity of the trustee/charity relationship when a trustee also becomes a service supplier to that charity. Further, the trustees should be mindful of the perceptions of third parties, donors, funders, members, volunteers and other supporters. The proposed arrangements may be lawful but will they be perceived as right and proper in the wider context?

2.5.9   Trustee remuneration/transactions – sections 67 and 68 of the Charities and Trustee Investment (Scotland) Act 2005

The legislation in Scotland begins with a general prohibition on remuneration of the trustees by a charity. The meaning of 'remuneration' is very wide, including any payments or benefits in kind:

- for being a charity trustee;

- in relation to a contract of employment with the charity;

- for other services to or on behalf of the charity.

It then provides a limited exception, allowing the *possibility* of remuneration for a minority of the trustees or others 'connected' with trustees for the provision of services to the charity. One of the important differences between these rules and those applicable under the Charities Act 2011 in England and Wales is that 'services' can include services as a charity trustee or as an employee, as well as other services and goods supplied in connection with services.

Connected persons include:

- spouses, civil partners, anyone a trustee is living with as husband or wife (or equivalent same sex relationship);

- children (this extends to those brought up or treated as children), stepchildren, grandchildren, parents, grandparents, brothers, sisters and spouses of any of those categories;

- institutions directly or indirectly controlled by a trustee or connected person;

- corporate bodies in which a trustee or connected person has a substantial interest (defined in section 105 of the Charities and Trustee Investment (Scotland) Act 2005);

- a Scottish partnership in which a trustee or connected person is a partner.

In order to come within this limited statutory exception, the situation must meet every one of the specified conditions. In summary they are:

1. The maximum amount of the remuneration must be set out in an agreement between the service provider and the charity.

2. That amount must be reasonable.

3. *Before* entering the agreement the trustees were satisfied that it would be in the charity's interests for those services to be provided by that service provider for that maximum sum.

4. Immediately *after* entering into the agreement, less than half the trustees can benefit from such arrangements (under this or other agreements).

5. The charity's governing document does not specifically prohibit the arrangement.

In addition, there are express exceptions to the main 'no remuneration' rule if there is an 'authorising provision' for remuneration due to any of these (see section 67(5) of the Charities and Trustee Investment (Scotland) Act 2005):

- a provision in the charity's governing document that was in force on or before 15 November 2004;

- an order of the Court of Session;

- any enactment (of the Scottish or UK Parliaments).

2.5.10   Trustee remuneration/transactions – sections 88–90 of the Charities Act (Northern Ireland) 2008

The new charity legislation in Northern Ireland provides a limited statutory authority for remuneration of trustees and connected persons for the provision of services to the charity. This is subject to four specific conditions and will only be available to the charity if its own constitution does not contain a specific prohibition on such arrangements. The trustees will also have an obligation to take into account guidance issued by the Charity Commission for Northern Ireland. At the date of preparation of this book these provisions have not yet been brought into force.

2.5.11   Trustees' indemnity insurance

The general 'no benefits' rule for charity trustees means that care must be taken with regard to trustees' indemnity insurance paid for out of charity funds. There is a specific statutory power for charities to fund such insurance *provided* there is no *specific* prohibition in the charity's governing document (see section 189 of the Charities Act 2011). If there is such a prohibition, specific permission must be obtained from the Charity Commission before arranging insurance cover at the charity's expense.

Whilst the legal possibility is open to charities, it is wise to think matters through properly before proceeding. A helpful checklist to follow is:

- Check the insurance cover already in place through the charity's own insurances – it may in fact already address some of the areas that are of concern to trustees.

- Isolate the areas of concern and identify whether they are actually about liabilities that would fall on the charity and its funds rather than on the trustees in their personal capacities.

- Does the charity's own legal form offer most of the protections that may in fact be lawful? (Eg the limited liability protection provided by a charitable company.)

- Consider the likelihood of relevant risks to trustees becoming a reality.

- Weigh up the costs against the limited potential benefits (bearing in mind the limitations in any permissible insurance cover) – is there real value?

- Consider how spending the charity's funds on the proposed insurance may be perceived by donors and other funders, members and beneficiaries.

- Check the constitution for possible specific prohibitions.

- Ensure the whole board discusses any proposal to arrange trustees' liability insurance. The decision should not be delegated to a sub-committee.

Trustees are, of course, entirely free to arrange personal insurance cover at their own expense – but they are hardly likely to be enthusiastic about doing so.

In Scotland, charity trustees now have a statutory power to arrange indemnity insurance funded by the charity (section 68A of the Charities and Trustee Investment (Scotland) Act 2005 as amended by the Public Services Reform (Scotland) Act 2010). Whilst this statutory power has effect notwithstanding any provision in the charity's constitution that prohibits personal benefits to trustees, it does not override any *express constitutional prohibition* on the purchase of relevant insurance.

The Scottish law permits insurance against personal liability for negligence, default or breach of duty by the charity trustees or directors or officers of any body carrying on activities on behalf of the charity. However, the cover cannot extend to criminal fines, regulatory penalties, legal costs of an unsuccessful defence of criminal proceedings or liabilities arising from conduct the trustee knew was not in the charity's interests. The same exclusion applies to conduct a trustee must reasonably be assumed to have known not to be in the charity's interests and where the trustee did not care whether the conduct was in the charity's interests.

2.5.12 Trustees' expenses

Reimbursement of genuine and reasonable out-of-pocket expenses incurred by trustees is permissible. This does not amount to remuneration of a trustee. There should, of course, be proper systems in place to make such reclaims and to ensure they are evidenced properly, and the evidence verified, by people other than the trustee in question. Expenses of the charity itself should not normally be paid by individual trustees and reclaimed. It is best practice for the organisation to deal directly with such payments – for example governance costs such as room hire for a board away day.

2.5.13 Transparency and disclosure requirements

Trustee-related transactions/remuneration/benefits/expenses

There will be various public disclosure and reporting requirements where there are any transactions with charity trustees or connected parties. These include obligations in *Accounting and Reporting by Charities: Statement of Recommended Practice, 2005* (SORP) (see www.charitycommission.gov.uk) to make disclosures in the annual accounts. For larger charities, that are subject to the full SORP requirements, if there has been no remuneration of trustees and no expenses paid to trustees those facts must be clearly stated.

Charities in the legal form of companies limited by guarantee also need to meet the company disclosure requirements of relevant accounting standards, such as the 'related party' transaction disclosure obligations.

Unsurprisingly, the charity regulators monitor annual accounts and other documents for such disclosures, not least to keep a watchful eye for any apparently unauthorised or otherwise improper transactions and payments. If there appears to be cause for concern they will make further enquiries of the relevant charity.

2.5.14   Trustees' liabilities – general

There are potential liabilities for trustees. For all trustees, in all legal forms of charities, these include:

*   criminal liabilities for breaches of specific general legal requirements;

*   criminal liabilities for breaches of specific charity law requirements;

*   personal civil liabilities for breaches of trust;

*   personal financial liabilities in the event of insolvency, where the trustees have failed to act properly before the insolvency.

2.5.15   Trustees' liabilities – particular legal forms of charities

For trustees in particular legal forms of charities, there are additional specific legal responsibilities, breaches of which may incur liabilities. Examples include:

*   directors' duties in charitable companies (or a trading subsidiary of any charity, whether or not that charity is a company);

*   specific duties and requirements concerning investments for the trustees of an unincorporated charity in England and Wales. These arise from the Trustee Act 2000. They are not obligatory for incorporated charities (eg charitable companies limited by guarantee).

- Charity law in Scotland imposes requirements regarding investments on all charities, regardless of their legal form (see the Charities and Trustee Investment (Scotland) Act 2005).

For trustees in unincorporated legal forms of charities (as is also the case when those forms are used for other not-for-profit activities) there is an inevitable personal responsibility and personal liability risk because of that legal form. Unincorporated organisations carry personal risks for their board members (whatever they may be called – committee members, trustees, etc). Those board members act in person when they commit to legal agreements, contracts and the like. Often they hold assets in their own names on behalf of the organisation. When disputes arise, it is the individuals who are at the sharp end in every sense. If the funds and assets of the organisation are inadequate to meet its debts and other liabilities, again the individuals are at personal risk.

2.6   Duties of company directors

Company law imposes duties on directors partly to recognise that they may have control of a company, the members of which are different people, but also to protect the interests of third parties dealing with the company and the interests of the wider community. Company law is not a devolved matter, unlike charity law. Therefore, the duties of directors apply to any company, registered in any part of the UK. (The Companies Act 2006 extends to the entire UK, companies in Northern Ireland are no longer subject to separate Northern Ireland specific company legislation.)

There are two groups of directors' duties:

- general duties; and

- specific duties (such as annual accounting and reporting obligations and the requirements to provide forms and documents to Companies House when certain events or transactions occur).

These duties apply to the directors of all companies, including directors of not-for-profit non-charitable companies, CICs and the trading subsidiaries of charities. They also apply to the trustees of charitable companies.

2.6.1   Directors' general duties – sections 171–177 of the Companies Act 2006

The general duties of directors (as they apply to non-commercial companies) are summarised here:

1. To act within the constitution and to exercise their powers for the purposes for which they were conferred.

2. To promote the success of the company in achieving its purposes (ie its 'objects').

3. To exercise independent judgement.

4. To exercise reasonable skill, care and diligence.

5. To avoid conflicts of interest.

6. Not to accept benefits from third parties.

7. To declare direct and indirect personal interests in proposed transactions or arrangements.

Much of the law regarding directors' general duties amounts to common sense and points out what should be both obvious and second nature in any charity or not-for-profit organisation, which exists for wider community purposes, not the immediate financial and material interests of its board and its legal members. Areas of the greatest likely complexity and challenge relate to conflicts of interest (see further comments below regarding duty 5).

In relation to duty 2, this is a modified version of the duty as it applies to the directors of companies whose objects are to benefit people other than their members. The directors of commercial companies are required to promote the 'success' of the company and, in doing so, take account of certain specified factors (such as the likely long-term consequences of decisions and the need to foster the company's business relationships). A not-for-profit company set up to actively promote its own members benefits would be subject to the duty in the unmodified form.

In relation to duty 3, the board members must not abrogate their responsibilities and simply do as others say. Equally, they must not fetter their own discretion to form opinions and make judgements. The board can certainly take advice and frequently should do, particularly from professional advisers in areas such as law, accounting and reporting, financial matters, tax and VAT. The board can also rely on the work of others, such as independent experts or consultants, or the expertise of the company's staff (or volunteers in many not-for-profit companies). What company law demands is that, having considered the advice or the relevant material, the board members then make their own judgement.

In relation to duty 4, the law looks at both:

- the general knowledge, skill and experience that can reasonably be expected of a person carrying out the functions of the director in that company (an objective test); and

- the general knowledge, skill and experience of the individual director (a subjective test).

Duty 5, to avoid conflicts, is potentially one of the most problematic. It is of particular importance in some CICs, for instance if their directors are paid employees or they or people/organisations connected to them invest in the CIC or have commercial or even semi-commercial links to it or dealings with it. Likewise, in some non-charitable not-for-profit companies there may be some personal commercial or other substantial material interests amongst the directors. In all such instances, it is important the potential problems of compliance with the company law rules are recognised. Equally, it is important that there is an active approach to identifying and dealing with all potentially harmful conflicts that arise in practice.

Duty 6 should pose no substantial problems in most charitable companies (and trading subsidiaries) because the general charity law principle remains that trustees must not receive any direct or indirect financial or other material benefit. However, where a particular charity permits remuneration or other benefits to trustees through specific provisions in its constitution or is relying on the limited statutory authority for certain transactions between trustees or connected persons and the charity (under the Charities Act 2006 or the Charities and Trustee Investment (Scotland) Act 2005 rules), care will need to be taken to address the Companies Act 2006 rules if that charity is in the legal form of a company (or if a trading subsidiary is involved). Provided the appropriate company law authority is put in place, alongside the relevant charity law authority, the matter can be properly addressed. It should certainly not be ignored.

It is important to recognise that duty 7 has a very wide impact. It relates to *proposed* transactions or arrangements. Broadly, any kind of interest, direct or indirect, must be disclosed, as must the nature and extent of that interest. So, interests of family members and businesses to which the director is connected would be relevant and would require declaration.

There are some exceptions. In particular, only matters the director is aware of or ought reasonably to be aware of must be declared and if something cannot reasonably be regarded as giving rise to a conflict of interest it is not strictly necessary to declare it. As a good rule of thumb and in the spirit of appropriate accountability and transparency that is of such importance in the third sector, it is better for a director to err on the side of caution in making declarations of interest.

The declaration needs to be made to the board as a whole and made *before* the company enters the transaction or arrangement. Where matters subsequently change or if the original declaration proves to be, or becomes, inaccurate or incomplete, a further declaration should be made. Clearly, given the importance of complying with directors' duties, such matters should be carefully and accurately documented and recorded.

The consequences of breaches of directors' duties generally include the possibility of damages or compensation for loss suffered by the company, restoration of company property, the making of an account to the company of any profits made by the director and, in cases where an interest in a contract was not disclosed, rescission of that contract. Where there is a breach of duty 4, the remedy for the company will be damages

A separate company law *obligation* (not a duty) exists to declare interests in *existing* transactions or arrangements (section 182 of the Companies Act 2006). The obligation is placed on the director and arises when that director becomes aware of a direct or indirect interest in a transaction or arrangement that has already been entered into by the company. The declaration required must be made to the board as soon as reasonably practicable and indicate the nature and extent of that interest. Failure to do so is a criminal offence.

2.6.2   Directors' duties – application to charity trustees

The general duties of directors apply to charity trustees if they are trustees of a charitable company or if they serve on the board of any charity's trading subsidiary. However, these company law duties should not cause them undue concern, given the high standards required of them under charity law. If they are competent in meeting their responsibilities in the charity law context, they will undoubtedly meet the company law standards expected of company directors.

2.6.3   Directors' duties – application to directors of community interest companies

Company law duties apply to the directors of CICs, including the general directors' duties summarised above. In addition, the directors of a CIC have a number of further and wider legal responsibilities, especially:

• To ensure the CIC delivers the particular community benefit for which it has been established.

• To ensure the CIC complies with the particular legal rules and restrictions that apply to CICs, including the relevant CIC regulations (these impose restrictions on matters such as benefits to and remuneration for directors, the use of the CIC's funds and assets, the levels of dividends that can be paid if the CIC has dividend bearing shares and limits on interest levels payable on some types of loan funding to CICs).

• To prepare and file the annual Community Interest Report (which should accompany the annual accounts and reports and is a public document).

• To ensure the CIC pays the relevant fee as it files that report.

2.6.4 Liabilities for breach of directors' general duties

Breaches of the general duties of directors can give rise to some or all of these potential civil liabilities:

• To account for sums received.

• To compensate the company for its losses.

• To restore the company's property.

• Where there has been failure to disclose an interest in a contract, that contract can be rescinded.

2.6.5 Indemnities and indemnity insurance for directors

Companies in general are permitted to arrange officers' liability insurance, including cover for their directors, and to fund the premiums from company funds (section 232(2) of the Companies Act 2006). This is a particular statutory exception to the Companies Act 2006 general ban on provisions that can exempt directors from liability (section 232 makes any attempt to do so void).

The exception states that a company can purchase and maintain for a director of the company, or any associated company, insurance against liability for:

• negligence;

• default;

• breach of duty; or

• breach of trust.

There are limitations on this statutory power and the insurance cover it might potentially be used to obtain, for instance there is a general legal principle that individuals cannot insure themselves against criminal liabilities for their own dishonesty. In addition, care should be taken to consider and address:

- the conflicts of interest that arise when a board is considering authorising insurance for its own benefit (the best approach is to ensure the articles specifically permit the board to authorise this particular form of benefit for directors);

- any relevant prohibitions in the company's own constitution (articles, or memorandum and articles in an older company);

- the limitations and exclusions in any proposed insurance policy;

- special considerations because of the type of company or the areas in which it operates – for example the limits on, and disclosure requirements regarding, benefits for CIC directors.

The position with regard to indemnity insurance for trustees of a charitable company is subject to particular charity law issues dealt with at para 2.5.11.

Non-charitable companies can potentially provide indemnities to their own directors for liabilities incurred by those directors to third parties. Strict conditions apply to such 'qualifying third party indemnity provisions' and there are public disclosure requirements (sections 234 and 236 of the Companies Act 2006).

Similar provisions permit indemnification with regard to liabilities of directors as trustees of occupational pension schemes. These are known as 'qualifying pension scheme indemnity provisions'. Again, strict conditions and public disclosure requirements must be met (sections 235 and 236 of the Companies Act 2006).

2.7   Honorary officers

Most charities and other not-for-profits will appoint some board members to hold particular positions within the board. These are often collectively termed the 'honorary officers'. The most common officer posts are chairman, deputy or vice-chairman, honorary treasurer and secretary or clerk. Whilst the holders of such offices may have particular responsibilities in the organisation, they should not act in general matters without reference to their board colleagues. The governance and the strategic management of the entity is a shared collective responsibility.

Eligibility to serve as officers (which may be limited to those who are current members of the organisation) and the mechanisms for appointing or electing people to the posts will normally be specified in the organisation's constitution. That document may also cover other matters such as the term of office and specific responsibilities – for example the chairman is usually required to chair all board meetings and any meetings of the members at which he or she is present. However, the detailed role and particular responsibilities of each office will usually be dealt with in standing orders or specific role descriptions authorised by the board. For model role descriptions for chairman, secretary and treasurer, see Appendix 1.

It remains common for a charity or other not-for-profit entity to have a secretary or equivalent role (eg clerk to the trustees in an unincorporated charitable trust). Under the Companies Act 2006 private companies, including charitable companies, are no longer required to have a company secretary, the position is optional. However, given the governance standards and accountability levels expected of charities and other not-for-profits, plus their heavier reporting and other public accountability obligations, it would be unwise for the board to dispense with the post.

Where a company's articles require the appointment of a secretary, that requirement must still be met. For other charities, it is often a requirement of the constitution that there be a secretary or clerk. Again, such a requirement must be met.

In large organisations, the secretary or clerk role may be a paid staff post. The role can be part of another post (eg finance director or administration manager) or it can be added to the responsibilities of the chief executive officer. In medium sized and smaller organisations it is much more likely to be a volunteer role. It is best for the secretary or clerk role to be undertaken as a dedicated 'stand alone' function, if possible, and it should be fulfilled by someone with sufficient expertise, knowledge and time to do justice to what are important responsibilities.

The overall purpose of a secretary or clerk post is to facilitate the good governance of the organisation, assist its compliance with relevant regulatory regimes, oversee its public accountability obligations and provide appropriate support to the board. The exact duties and functions will, however, vary considerably from one organisation to another, because of the diversity in purposes (objects), activities, size and legal nature. Besides having oversight of the governance systems, the responsibilities will often also include internal administration.

The likely core duties and common associated duties of a secretary or clerk are set out below.

2.7.1   Core duties

- Issuing notices, agenda and papers for meetings.

- Attending trustee and general meetings and taking minutes.

- Acting as correspondent for the board.

- Taking custody of registers, minute books and records.

- Certifying returns to statutory authorities.

- Handling other statutory compliance (eg notifications to Companies House, the Charity Commission, the OSCR and other regulators).

- Taking custody of the seal and supervising its use (if the organisation has a seal).

- Being the custodian of the governing document (ie retaining custody of the physical item but also ensuring the terms of the governing document are known, understood and followed, as well as periodically arranging review and updating of that document).

2.7.2   Common associated duties

- Advising on governance matters.

- Providing and/or obtaining legal advice.

- Supporting, training and development of trustees.

- Assisting with or facilitating some or all of the following:
  - property matters (including intellectual property);
  - insurance;
  - office management;
  - health and safety;
  - data protection;
  - personnel;
  - accounting and tax matters;
  - procedures for contracting and entering into other major legal agreements.

2.8   The governing document

The constitution of an organisation is its governing document. It sets the framework within which that organisation is governed. It may (and *must*, in the case of a charity or CIC) set limited purposes ('objects') and specify controls on how the funds and assets can be used and on what would happen to final funds in the event of the organisation being wound up.

If the organisation has a formal legal membership, the constitution should address eligibility for membership, the mechanism by which people apply for and are admitted to membership, the key rights and responsibilities of the members and, of course, how and when membership ceases.

An organisation must normally act within its own constitution. Its governing body should ensure it does so and must manage the entity and its affairs in accordance with that constitution. Failure to do so properly in a company or charity can be a breach of the legal duties of directors or trustees. The governing body must also ensure others involved in the organisation follow the constitution – including any members of a body that has a formal legal membership.

In most cases, the constitution will deal with the appointment of the governing body itself and, to some extent, provide it with suitable powers to manage the entity. Both those areas are also subject to wider legal rules, such as:

- the legal criteria for disqualification of company directors;

- the legal criteria for disqualification of charity trustees (which include disqualification from directorship);

- the charitable trusts of a charity;

- the general statutory duties of directors;

- applicable specific statutory duties of directors (eg to ensure a company annual return is filed at Companies House each year);

- the general duties of charity trustees;

- applicable specific statutory duties of charity trustees (eg in relation to public accounting and reporting; investments; disposal of land and charging of charity property (England and Wales));

- applicable specific statutory duties of the trustees of a CIO or SCIO or the directors of a CIC.

2.8.1   Company constitutions

The articles constitute the key governance document for a company. They take precedence over any other governance-related documents the individual company may choose to adopt (such as rules or bye-laws or standing orders for the conduct of meetings). However, where the articles conflict with mandatory rules in the Companies Act 2006 it is the legislation that takes precedence. For example, if the articles attempt to prevent the use of proxies or attempt to restrict a member's choice of who acts as proxy for that member at a general meeting, that will be ineffective because company members have an absolute right to use a proxy of their choice.

2.8.2   Community interest company constitutions

General company law rules on constitutions apply to CIC constitutions, so they too use articles of association. However it should be noted that the relevant statutory provisions specific to CICs require additional restrictions in their constitutions, because of the community benefit obligations of CICs and the 'asset lock' that applies to them. It is not permissible for a CIC's constitution to override the compulsory obligations and limitations of the CIC legislation.

2.8.3   Charitable incorporated organisation and Scottish charitable incorporated organisation constitutions

There are specific legal requirements for the constitutions of CIOs and SCIOs. The framework is set out in the Charities Act 2006 for CIOs (England and Wales) and the Charities and Trustee Investment (Scotland) Act 2005 for SCIOs (Scotland), with further details in relevant regulations.

2.8.4   Unincorporated association constitutions

By way of contrast, there are no statutory provisions in relation to the constitutions of unincorporated associations. This is essentially because there is no specific statutory framework for unincorporated associations, which operate in a much looser common law setting.

The clarity and adequacy of an unincorporated association's constitution are therefore of particular importance. Unfortunately, many constitutions fail to deliver properly in both areas.

2.9   How governance is actually done

Governance needs procedures for its delivery. These are the mechanics of governance, such as the organisation's structures, its internal decision-making procedures, its monitoring and communications processes and so on.

In the case of a charity, its trustees are in essence stewards and custodians of the charity, its funds and assets, its charitable purposes, the public benefit it provides and its good standing and reputation. So, their approach to practical governance and the day-to-day management and operation of that charity must be appropriate to that important legal setting.

Key issues that affect the practical delivery of governance and the strategic management of a charity or not-for-profit entity include:

• what legal form the organisation takes and the legal consequences of that;

• the contents of the organisation's own constitution;

• the size and scale of the organisation and the nature and scope of its activities.

2.9.1   Legal structures for governance and governance models

Companies and CICs are inherently two-level organisations in terms of their legal structure – they have directors (who are, collectively, the governing body) and formal legal members. It is quite permissible for the same group of people to hold both roles and this often occurs in small organisations.

However, company law is structured from the premise that the board may be acting on behalf of a much wider membership. It therefore provides members with certain legal rights that are absolute – the company's constitution cannot remove them and its board cannot prevent their exercise (such as the right to receive annual accounts and reports or to exercise voting rights at general meetings in person or by proxy). Company law also provides a range of 'checks and balances' designed, at least in part, to ensure the members' interests and their legal membership rights are protected. So, there is an ultimate statutory power for members to remove directors (subject to strict procedures) and a voluntary winding up requires a formal members' decision.

This provides a clear legal role for the directors compared to the members and imposes both general and specific legal limits beyond which directors cannot go. General limits are found in areas such as directors' duties, whereas specific limits are set by requirements of the Companies Act 2006 for members' authority or members' decisions on particular matters. In this way, company law reserves certain matters to the members of a company – a checklist of the most important of these is set out below.

2.9.2 Companies – checklist of matters reserved to the members

A company incorporated under company legislation, including a CIC, must pass formal members' resolutions to deal with these matters. This is not an exhaustive list, rather it highlights some of the more common events/transactions where a members' decision will be required. A special resolution is necessary, unless otherwise stated. Items that only apply to share companies, such as trading subsidiaries) are indicated:

- Removing carried forward share capital restrictions from a company incorporated before 1 October 2009 (share companies). For example the limit on authorised share capital or the directors' authority to allot shares. (Such an authority was previously required for private share companies under section 80 of the Companies Act 1985.) This requires an ordinary resolution. (These restrictions do not apply to companies incorporated on or after 1 October 2009 under the Companies Act 2006.)

- Share capital changes, such as consolidation, subdivision, redenomination (share companies). The type of resolution required varies, depending on factors such as the precise proposed change and the terms of the current articles.

- Change of name (unless the articles permit a change by other means, such as a resolution of the directors).

- Changes to the articles. This includes changes to any provisions of the memorandum of association of a company incorporated before 1 October 2009 (those provisions are now deemed part of its articles, for instance the company's objects).

- Changes to the rights of classes of members (guarantee companies) or share class rights (share companies). Class consents from the members in the relevant class are required. There are various ways in which those can be obtained.

- Members' voluntary winding up.

Unincorporated associations are actually unincorporated *members'* associations, so they also have two groups of people involved – the governing body and the membership. In practice, the people involved frequently fail to recognise the distinction between the two roles (as also happens with companies). The problems that arise when clarity is not maintained are, to a certain extent, worse than would be the case for a company structure because the law relating to unincorporated associations is far less comprehensive and often less clear or certain.

2.9.3 Matters reserved to the members – unincorporated associations

Certain matters are normally reserved to the members in unincorporated associations (typically changes to the organisation's name or constitution and the voluntary dissolution of the organisation). However, unlike companies operating under company law, there is no statutory framework that specifies what must be dealt with at membership level. So, *what* matters are reserved to the members of an unincorporated association depends heavily on the individual organisation's constitution.

2.9.4 Governance 'models'

Subject to the overarching legal structure and consequential legal rules that apply because of the organisation's legal form, there is some flexibility in what governance 'model' an organisation may choose to adopt (ie how it actually organises who its members and board are). Common models are:

- *flat model* – exactly the same people serve on the governing body as are the members of the organisation;

- *membership model* – a wider circle of people become members, with full member-level voting and other rights, with a smaller group appointed to the board;

- *hybrid model* – limited rights for the wider group, with the smaller group taking on the responsibilities of the board.

The flat model suits a small organisation or a body such as a grant making trust that wants to offer limited liability protection for its trustees (so uses the legal form of a company limited by guarantee rather than an unincorporated trust).

The membership model suits larger organisations and those that depend on a wider membership for funds, to engage with and influence third parties and to provide a source of volunteers.

A hybrid model may be useful where different levels of involvement are desirable or appropriate for certain interest groups. So, a social or sports club will often have recreational or temporary membership options. A charity may introduce a range of membership classes to cater for different specialist needs and interests (eg family membership) or to increase income (eg from corporate member subscriptions). Care must be taken to distinguish those who have formal legal membership from others involved in a different capacity (eg as supporters or associates, or service users involved in a consultative committee or advisory group).

If different membership classes with different rights are introduced, the constitution needs to be well drafted and, in the case of a company, all changes to membership class rights and even changes to the names of membership classes require notification to Companies House under rules introduced by the Companies Act 2006. Variation of existing rights also requires the consent of the members in that class (sections 638–640 of the Companies Act 2006).

2.9.5   Keeping things practical

As in many areas of life, reality is often rather different from theory in the governance and management of charities and not-for-profits. Most organisations in the charity and not-for-profit sectors are very tiny, with limited funds, scarce resources and few, if any, paid employees. People usually hold multiple roles and the organisation probably operates quite informally. Few of the board members are likely to have any legal, accounting or financial management knowledge, and practical experience of such areas will also be a rarity. Volunteers serving on that governing body will be doing so in their own time, often fitting the demands of leading a charity or not-for-profit organisation around family responsibilities, employment, other forms of public or community service and much else.

Keeping things in perspective is therefore important:

- Approximately a million people act as volunteer charity trustees in the UK.

- The charity sector in England and Wales receives £53 billion income annually, it spends £51 billion in activities that benefit those in greatest need and benefit society as a whole.

- Charities care for £52.2 billion worth of community assets.

- Only around 6% of charities have income over £500,000 and 75% of the registered charities in England and Wales have annual income *below* £100,000.

- In Scotland, 82% of charities have income below £100,000 a year.

(*Source*: Charity Commission/OSCR.)

2.9.6   Making the right choices

To provide a *good governance framework*, the right choices need to be made for that particular organisation. To *deliver* good governance, within the relevant compulsory legal framework and those chosen options, the organisation's governance framework needs to be followed in practice and operated well.

The board ought to think through key areas, when deciding its approach to governance, including:

- The organisation's fundamental purposes (often described as its 'objects'), as set out in its constitution. They are the organisation's *raison d'etre* and affect every aspect of it. In the case of a charity, ensuring the charitable purposes are effectively pursued is one of the board's most important roles.

- What wider values the organisation has, or should have, and what the impact of those values is in relation to how the organisation is or ought to be governed. Values adopted and all expressions of those values, such as 'mission statements', must support the organisation's purposes and be consistent with them – beware 'mission drift'!

- What governance regime the organisation's present constitution specifies. The organisation cannot generally ignore rules in its own constitution.

- Any additional governance procedures that have been or could be voluntarily adopted – there may be standing orders or rules and bye-laws that set out details of procedures to be followed at board meetings for example.

Individuals serving on a governing body may not recognise their own role and responsibilities. All too often, they are not aware that they are directors or the equivalent in an unincorporated organisation, such as committee members in a members' association.

This can be the fault of the organisation's recruitment and appointment processes. An invitation along the lines of 'We'd like you to help Nempnett Thrubwell Sports Club, the AGM's on Saturday evening at 7' is not uncommon. The invitee would be unlikely to grasp immediately the potential legal consequences of that invitation to stand for appointment to the board.

Failure to grasp the basics of the governance role may in part be due to the terminology used, either in the constitution or by the board itself in its proceedings and its records. Third sector organisations often describe their governing body as a 'management committee' or 'council', rather than a board. The governing body is responsible for the governance of the entity, whatever the governing body may be called. Whatever term is used, it should be used consistently throughout the organisation. It should also be in line with the wording of the constitution, to avoid another source of doubt and confusion.

2.9.7   Start as you mean to go on – engaging new board members

It is wise to have at least an informal discussion with potential candidates who are considering standing for appointment to the governing body, about the general nature of the organisation and of the role (for instance, that it is a charitable company and the role is that of director and charity trustee). It is also best to make them aware of any specific expectations, such as the number of meetings they will need to attend, when and where those are held, whether board members are also expected to serve on sub-committees, attend strategic planning away days and so on.

Potential candidates should always be made aware that they are being asked to take on legal responsibilities *before* they are formally proposed for appointment. Providing them with a copy of the role description for a board member of the particular organisation should be the norm. They should also be equipped with basic key documents about the organisation, to help them decide whether or not to offer their time and talents in this particular way (at the least, its constitution and its most recent annual accounts and reports).

If the candidacy proceeds and an appointment is made, as an absolute minimum the new board member should be provided with:

- a basic induction programme;

- a schedule of meetings for the year to come;

- confirmation of his or her role and responsibilities (for specimen role descriptions, see Appendix 1);

- minutes of at least the last three board meetings.

Depending on the nature of the organisation, it may be appropriate to address other matters, such as IT remote access authority, email and intranet facilities, visits to key sites or programmes, meeting senior staff and/or lead volunteers, introduction to key partner organisations or umbrella bodies/regional and national associated bodies.

2.9.8   Supporting the board

Wherever possible, ongoing support should be offered to board members. This can include board training and development, perhaps with external facilitation; mentoring; and encouraging board members to join relevant voluntary sector networks and support groups (eg the trustee network support encouraged by the Small Charities Coalition).

A short, simple governance handbook is a very helpful tool for board members (but a long and complex one is not). Its contents should include the constitution, at least the preceding year's public accounts and reports, the role descriptions for board members and each principal officer (chairman, secretary or clerk to the trustees, treasurer or finance trustee, etc) and the terms of reference of sub-committees.

If the governance handbook can be made available in an electronic form, with remote access facilities for board members, using it will be easier (and so will the task of updating it). The possibility of people following out-of-date procedures or relying on superseded documents will also be reduced. Costs may also be less than they would be if hard copies had to be printed and distributed and the organisation's environmental impact may also be reduced.

2.10   Delegation by charity trustees

The trustees of a charity can delegate the exercise of specified powers on the charity's behalf and the carrying out of particular activities or functions. They cannot delegate their trusteeship and the discharge of its responsibilities.

This is subject to the charity's constitution empowering the trustees to delegate and provided there is no statutory restriction on the particular delegation proposed. Note that there are particular controls over the delegation of discretionary investment powers. Those controls are statutory and are relevant to unincorporated charities in England and Wales and to all charities in Scotland. See the Trustee Act 2000 with regard to England and Wales, and the Charities and Trustee Investment (Scotland) Act 2005 with regard to charities on the Scottish Charity Register.

The individual rules in the particular constitution must be observed in relation to all delegation. For example there may be rules about the establishment, size and composition of a committee and specific requirements with regard to the subsequent conduct of its meetings and exercise of its delegated authority. Particular care should be taken about restrictions on the delegation of expenditure decisions and powers to bind the charity or commit it to legal agreements, including but not limited to contracts.

Any delegation does not remove the collective and individual responsibilities of the trustees. They must supervise the body to which they have delegated powers and monitor the exercise of those powers.

Regular and appropriate reporting and provision of information back to the trustees is key as part of the monitoring/supervision process. Clear and accurate records of the original delegation, any subsequent changes to it and of the activities of the body to which it was made should also be maintained. That will include minutes of board meetings and sub-committee meetings.

It is essential that there is clarity over exactly what has been delegated and what the delegated body can and cannot therefore do (eg whether it can incur expenditure on the charity's behalf and, if so, under what conditions and subject to what financial limits). It is therefore good practice for committees and sub-committees to operate under written terms of reference approved by the board. These should be reviewed and updated periodically.

2.10.1 Delegation to staff

Charities and other not-for-profits may engage staff. The staff members have delegated authority in the context of their specific roles. They are accountable through the chain of management to the board via the chief executive (or comparable senior staff member).

It is important to distinguish clearly between the delegated authority of employed staff (evidenced in job descriptions, internal procedures and policies, standing instructions or orders, working procedures, etc) and the strategic role and ultimate legal responsibilities of the trustees.

It is equally important for the board to monitor the staff and the manner in which they exercise their delegated authority, as part of the board's overall responsibility to monitor the entire organisation. However, the temptation for the board to 'micro-manage' must be resisted, remembering that their focus is on strategy, policy and the overall well-being of the organisation.

Open communication should be maintained between the board and staff. There should also be adequate information flows between both groups.

2.10.2 Delegation to volunteers

In many cases a charity or other not-for-profit is heavily or even entirely dependent on volunteers to carry out the activities and deal with the day-to-day management and administration. The same legal principles relating to delegation by the board, and its responsibilities to oversee and monitor those volunteers to whom particular functions and responsibilities have been delegated, apply in the context of staff. There are particular practical challenges in dealing with all of that when unpaid volunteers are involved, often operating at some physical distance from the trustees and any premises the charity may have.

There should be at least basic documentation in place, such as a volunteers' code of practice. It is advisable to have written role descriptions for key volunteers, bearing in mind that employment terminology for such items (eg 'job description') is not appropriate and should be avoided.

2.10.3   Reporting lines

It is important that reporting lines are clear and understood by those to whom delegated powers have been given and by the board which has authorised the delegation. These are typical examples in various sizes of organisation.

Reporting lines in a large or medium sized organisation

Board

↑

Chief executive officer

↑

Senior management team

↑

Staff and volunteers

There may be some overlap between the active volunteer team and the board members.

Particular members of the senior management team may have specific responsibilities in relation to the recruitment, development, deployment and management of volunteers.

Reporting lines in a medium sized organisation

Board

↑

Chief executive officer

↑

Staff and volunteers

There is likely to be considerable overlap between the active volunteer team and the board members. The staff team will probably be quite small.

Reporting lines in a small organisation

Board

↑

Volunteers

In small organisations there are unlikely to be any paid staff and the board and volunteers may be the same people.

3 Membership

3.1 What is 'membership'?

Many, but not all, organisations have a formal membership, in addition to the membership of their governing body. This chapter examines some of the important legal and practical issues relating to such formal legal members – the people who are the 'true' members of a charity or other not-for-profit organisation.

Certain legal forms commonly used by charities and not-for-profits inherently require a legal membership – for example an unincorporated members' association or a company limited by guarantee. Other legal forms do not permit formal membership, they simply have a governing body – the most common example is an unincorporated charitable trust, which only has trustees.

It is essential to identify whether or not a particular organisation has a formal membership. There are both legal and practical implications, including these examples:

- Members will have some rights and responsibilities.

- Decisions must be taken by the right group of people in order to be valid and effective.

- Individuals on the governing body need to know when they are acting in that capacity as they have legal responsibilities and potential liabilities.

- There may be overriding applicable statutory rules relating to members and membership (this is particularly the case in relation to companies).

3.1.1 Legal forms that require membership

The following legal forms inherently require a membership:

- companies limited by guarantee;

- CICs;

- industrial and provident societies;

- corporate bodies incorporated by Royal Charter;

- CIOs and SCIOs;

- unincorporated members' associations.

A specific organisation in one of the above legal forms may have a general, public membership, or it may have structured itself so that its only members are those serving on its governing body.

3.1.2 Informal 'membership'

Some charities and not-for-profits have groups of people described as 'members' who are not in fact formal members in any legal sense. Rather, they are in some other, less formal, relationship with the organisation, such as belonging to a supporters' group that provides volunteers, other practical support, or perhaps funding through regular or occasional donations.

Considerable difficulties and even legal risks arise if organisations fail to distinguish between their formal legal members and people in other categories (who may be called 'members' but in fact are not). The constitution should be well worded, to demonstrate the different categories and the different relationships they have with the entity. It is best practice to avoid the word 'member' for any group of people not intended to be formal legal members. Clear and accurate record-keeping also helps avoid problems (well worded minutes, accurate and up-to-date records of the formal legal members in a membership register, and so forth).

3.1.3 Members of companies limited by guarantee

The Companies Act 2006 permits a guarantee company to have just one member, subject to the company's articles – in a charitable company at least three is the normal minimum. Each member has personal membership rights and responsibilities in the company but no property ownership attaching to their membership, as there are no shareholdings.

3.1.4 Members of companies limited by shares

A private company limited by shares must have at least one member under the Companies Act 2006 (though the articles may require two or more as a minimum in the particular company). Each member is a shareholder, holding at least one share. Trading subsidiaries of charities are typically limited by shares.

3.1.5 Members of community interest companies

A member of a CIC limited by shares will have a shareholding, whereas a guarantee CIC member has personal membership rights but no shareholding.

3.1.6 Role of members in companies

The role of members in a charitable or not-for-profit company is largely passive. Having provided the payment on their shares, which helps fund the company's business activities (alongside its borrowings), they take no part in the strategic management of the company. That is the responsibility of the board of directors. The same is true of members in a CIC.

3.1.7 Financial interests of members – share companies

In a company or CIC limited by shares, the members have a financial interest, as part owners of the company or CIC, according to the number of shares they hold. What, if any, financial return they get on that interest, in the normal annual cycle of the business, depends on whether:

- the share class they hold carries any dividend rights; and
- the company makes sufficient 'distributable profits' to provide a surplus, beyond the projected future business needs, that can fund a dividend payment.

The Companies Act 2006 imposes rules about what sources of funds can be regarded as distributable profits and how the directors of a share company determine the levels of such profits. More restrictive rules apply to CICs.

In most cases where a company limited by shares, rather than a company limited by guarantee, is operating in the voluntary sector (rather than the social enterprise sector), dividends are unlikely to be paid.

Members disposing of their shares by sale may also gain financial benefit from any increase in the capital value of their shares. This can only occur in individual companies where the articles permit transfer of shares by way of commercial private sale.

A charity that has a trading subsidiary normally extracts the surplus profits from that company by means of an annual donation from the subsidiary to the charity under the Gift Aid scheme (not by dividend payments).

3.2   Membership – legal capacity

There are certain underlying legal principles which affect basic legal capacity to be a member of an organisation, especially a company or similar corporate body. Legal capacity is the key issue for company membership. A 'person' in law has that capacity.

Generally, a 'person' in law is an individual with full legal capacity or an organisation that has its own recognised legal capacity, distinct from the individuals who are part of that organisation. An example of an organisation with legal capacity (often called legal identity) is a private limited company. Individuals normally have legal capacity if they are of adult age and nothing has removed their rights and capacity to exercise control over their own affairs (such as certain mental health protective orders or personal bankruptcy).

Organisations that do *not* have legal capacity, such as an unincorporated members' association, cannot strictly take membership of other organisations and so cannot become members of companies. A charitable company may want to have unincorporated organisations in a membership relationship with the charity, for instance if the charitable company is an umbrella body for other organisations, or a national body providing central coordination or support to local organisations. The technical legal difficulty can be overcome through appropriate clauses in the company's articles of association. For example, provisions could:

• allow relevant unincorporated organisations to nominate an adult individual to apply for membership of the charity (effectively acting on behalf of their organisation); or

• permit one of the current officers of specified organisations to become members of the charitable company.

3.3   Membership – eligibility

In order to determine who can be a member of an organisation it is important to consider eligibility. Such eligibility criteria should be distinguished from the administrative and legal processes by which eligible people become or cease to be members (ie the mechanics of admission to membership).

Some factors affecting eligibility flow from the wider law and others from the specific organisation's own constitution. Wider legal issues include the legal capacity of the potential member (as discussed above) and specific legal bars that may inhibit a particular individual or organisation from becoming a member. Specific legal bars are less likely to arise in the context of membership than they are in the context of becoming a member of a governing body (in the latter, legal bars to directorship or trusteeship arise in a number of situations). However, eligibility criteria arising from the constitution are far more common.

3.3.1 Membership – constitutional eligibility

The organisation's own constitution may include rules about eligibility for membership. If it does, care should be taken to ensure any applicant for membership meets the particular criteria. Suitable evidence should be obtained and checked before the application is granted.

The detail of the eligibility criteria varies widely from one organisation to another. In a professional body, and in many specialist medical and scientific bodies, detailed requirements regarding skills and qualifications are likely to apply. There may also be required standards of conduct and adherence to ethical codes or similar requirements. By contrast, membership of a sports-related organisation may be dependent on participation in a particular sport.

Charities with wider public memberships than their trustee board may have quite simple criteria, based on support of their charitable purposes and basic legal capacity, in order to encourage the greatest level of membership support from the public.

3.4 Membership – guarantee companies

The legal members of a company limited by guarantee are the persons listed in the company's register of members. The initial members are the 'subscribers' who agree to become members on incorporation. These persons are listed in the memorandum provided to the Registrar of Companies as part of the incorporation process.

Guarantee company members have personal rights and responsibilities with regard to their membership but do not own shares, as guarantee companies do not have a share capital.

The members are protected by limited liability through the mechanism of their guarantee, which limits their potential liability to contribute towards the debts and other liabilities of the company to a fixed monetary sum (typically just £1). The liability lasts for a year after cessation of membership. It should be noted that the guarantee only becomes operative if a liquidator calls for payment, in the event of the company's insolvency.

A guarantee company may have different classes of members, with different rights attaching to each class. The differences may be largely practical, such as different levels of membership subscriptions for retired members compared to working age members. However, it may relate to fundamental matters of company membership, such as voting rights. As a rule of thumb, a matter relevant to fundamental company law rights should be addressed in the articles (eg that a particular category of membership cannot vote at general meetings). Lower level matters, such as differences in membership subscriptions, can be addressed in rules and bye-laws, outside the articles.

Reforms introduced by the Companies Act 2006 provide protections for the rights of guarantee company members where any variation of those rights is proposed. Previous company legislation only addressed the variation of share class rights in companies limited by shares. As a result, there are now public filing requirements for guarantee companies when new membership classes are created or the names of existing classes altered and when the rights of any membership class are changed.

3.5   Membership – share companies

A private company limited by shares must have at least one member. That person is a shareholder, who will hold at least one share.

Where a charity operates a trading subsidiary, that subsidiary is likely to be limited by shares. If the charity is in a legal form capable of doing so (eg it is a charitable company), it will hold the share in its own right and be entered in the subsidiary's register of members under its own name as the shareholder. If it cannot hold the share itself, for example because it is in an unincorporated legal form, then it must use slightly cumbersome legal and administrative arrangements to hold the share through a human nominee.

3.6   Membership – community interest companies

As CICs are a particular type of company, their initial members are the subscribers notified to Companies House at incorporation in the memorandum. Subsequently, membership depends on being listed as a member in the register of members. Whether the members of a CIC are simply members or are shareholders depends on whether the CIC is limited by guarantee or by shares.

3.7 Members' rights

Members have rights which may flow from the organisation's own constitution or may be statutory rights. The source of the rights, and the extent to which they can be varied or restricted, largely depends on the legal form the particular organisation takes.

3.7.1 Members' rights – unincorporated members' associations

Unincorporated members' associations are essentially governed by common law, not statute. There are few inherent rights of members in unincorporated associations. Rather, the rights are heavily dependent on the terms of the particular organisation's own constitution. Many constitutions are poorly worded in this respect, leading to uncertainty about who the legal members are, leaving membership rights unclear or giving apparently contradictory rights in different clauses of the constitution. This often leads to difficulties in both the practical operation of the organisation and in its legal administration. The difficulties can be particularly severe if disputes arise amongst the members, or between some of the members and the committee.

3.7.2 Members' rights – companies

In the case of companies, including CICs, members' rights are both statutory and constitutionally based. Significant rights arise from company law, in particular the Companies Act 2006. Important examples include the following rights:

1. To attend, speak and vote at general meetings of the members (unless the particular membership class held has restrictions in these matters, imposed by the company's articles).

2. To appoint a proxy of the member's choice to attend, speak and vote at any general meeting on the appointing member's behalf.

3. To vote on written resolutions (provided the member is an 'eligible member' in relation to the particular resolution (see para 3.14.2)).

4. To receive copies of the annual accounts and reports of the company.

Note that item 1 is subject to the specific rights of the individual class of membership held by the member in question. The articles should set out clearly any restrictions, for instance that a particular class of members have restricted voting rights or no voting rights.

Unless the membership class held has no voting rights at all, a member can always exercise his statutory right to appoint a proxy. This right cannot be removed or restricted by provisions in the company's articles (as was once the case under previous company law). So, any clause that attempts to restrict the choice of proxy (eg that only another member of the company can be appointed) is ineffective. Such out-of-date provisions should be removed by altering the articles, to avoid confusion and accidental infringement of members' rights.

Items 3 and 4 cannot be restricted or removed by provisions in the articles, they are absolute rights.

Collectively, members also have particular rights in relation to matters reserved to the members, which the board cannot deal with. The Companies Act 2006 deliberately gives the members the power to make certain decisions, important examples include:

- A special resolution of the members is required to alter the articles or change the company's name (in the latter case, unless the articles give a specific power to the directors to alter the name, which is rare).

- A director can be removed from office *as a director* by ordinary resolution of the members in general meeting (this cannot be done by written resolution).

- The auditor can be removed by an ordinary resolution of the members in general meeting, before the end of his or her period of office.

Special notice must be given of any proposed resolution to remove a director or the auditor and other detailed procedural requirements apply. The director or auditor has various rights, including the right to attend and speak at the relevant general meeting.

Forcible removal of a director is a serious and potentially risky matter, so appropriate legal advice should always be taken before embarking upon such a course of action. Note that the employment of an employed director cannot be terminated simply by removing him or her from the office of director. Appropriate employment law compliant procedures must be followed to terminate that employment.

3.7.3 Members' rights – charitable incorporated organisations and Scottish charitable incorporated organisations

Members' rights in CIOs and SCIOs are broadly comparable to the rights of members in a charitable company. Some rights flow from the relevant legislation, whilst others depend on the constitution of the particular CIO or SCIO. CIO and SCIO members also have certain legal duties (see para 3.12.4).

3.7.4 Variation of members' rights

Requirements and procedures for variation of members' rights in an unincorporated members' association will largely depend on the individual organisation's constitution.

In companies the variation of members' rights is subject to Companies Act 2006 requirements. There are statutory provisions for variation of rights in both share and guarantee private companies (including CICs).

Rights attaching to shares may only be varied:

(a) in accordance with the variation of rights provisions in the articles; or

(b) where the articles do not include such provisions, if the holders of the class give consent (section 630 of the Companies Act 2006).

That consent can be given either:

(a) in writing from the holders of at least three-quarters in nominal value of the issued shares in the class of shares; or

(b) by a special resolution passed at a separate meeting of the holders of the class of shares.

The variation of the rights of a class of members in a guarantee company also requires advance consent (section 631 of the Companies Act 2006). As with share companies, if the articles provide a variation method that must be followed, otherwise class consents must be obtained by one of these methods:

(a) in writing from the holders of at least three-quarters of the members in that class; or

(b) by a special resolution passed at a separate meeting of the holders of the class of shares.

The courts have taken a wide view of what is a 'variation' of rights, whether it is a direct or indirect variation. In addition, the Companies Act 2006 specifically provides that any change to the articles with regard to variation of rights is itself a variation of class rights. It is advisable to take a cautious view and obtain consents if there is any possibility of a proposed matter being a variation of rights.

In addition, guarantee companies must notify the Registrar of Companies when they:

(a)   create a new class of members (form SH11); or

(b)   give a name to, or change the name of, a membership class (form SH13); or

(c)   vary the rights of a class of members (form SH12).

A share company that varies share class rights must notify the Registrar by submitting form SH10.

3.8   Members' liabilities

Apart from their liability with regard to their shareholdings or guarantee, members of companies are generally protected from personal liability with regard to their company's day-to-day activities and the company's debts and other liabilities. The position is far less certain in an unincorporated members' association. For further comments regarding the legal doubts and difficulties, see Chapter 1.

3.9   Admission of new members

The process by which a person becomes a member depends on the wider law, the legal form of the particular organisation (eg a company limited by guarantee or an unincorporated members' association) and that organisation's own constitution. For unincorporated organisations, the constitution is the main consideration. For companies, the articles of the individual company are important but there are also company law procedures and requirements to address.

Eligibility rules applicable to the individual organisation always need to be considered before embarking on a process to admit a new member.

Some organisations require an admission fee and/or a first year's annual subscription to be paid by an applicant for membership. This is common in unincorporated members' associations and guarantee companies that are charities or not-for-profit organisations.

3.9.1   Admission of new members – unincorporated members' associations

The constitution of the particular organisation should be checked to see how admissions of new members are dealt with. Particular care is needed to establish which group of people has the power to admit applicants. It may be the committee or other governing body but in some cases applications will need to be determined by decision of the current membership at the annual general meeting (AGM).

A typical process, found in many constitutions, is:

- application by the prospective member (usually on an approved style of application form used by that particular organisation);

- a formal decision on the application by the relevant group of people (eg the governing body).

Some organisations will allow discretion over the granting of the application but in many, provided the applicant meets the eligibility requirements of the membership class applied for, and duly pays any admission fee or first year's subscription, the application cannot be refused. Note that a CASC must have open membership (this is a condition for CASC tax benefits).

Whilst there are no specific legal rules governing records of membership applications, decisions taken on them and the actual admission of a new member, it is common sense that all of this should be clearly and accurately documented. Equally, a proper list of members should be maintained at all times, with up-to-date information about all current members. Many membership charities experience difficulties as a result of incomplete or inaccurate membership records and such difficulties can be severe.

3.9.2 Admission of new members – companies in general

The admission of new members to companies is subject to the Companies Act 2006 rules and requirements, as well as the individual company's articles. There are some important differences between companies limited by guarantee and companies limited by shares.

3.9.3 Admission of new members – companies limited by guarantee

The first ever members of a guarantee company are determined by automatic legal process. As the certificate of incorporation is issued by the Registrar of Companies and the company comes into existence as a legal entity, the people who agreed to be the 'subscribers' on the memorandum become the first members. Their details should be entered in the register of members of the company as soon as practicable (and by law the entry must be made within a maximum of 2 months) but they already are legal members from that moment of incorporation. Note that the binding legal guarantee towards payment of the company's debts and liabilities, on any future winding up, is also automatic – the first members become subject to that guarantee as the company is incorporated.

Subsequent admissions of new members require certain administrative and legal steps to be taken, which always include:

- consent to membership from the applicant;
- entry of the new member in the register of members (it is when this occurs that the person becomes a legal member of the company).

It is very likely that the company's articles will also require a written membership application in a particular form. This can be a useful mechanism to ensure any admission fee or first year's membership subscription is paid and to obtain signed evidence of consent to membership and its consequent responsibilities (such as complying with the articles, which are the constitution of the company).

In many companies, the board of directors must make a specific decision on applications for membership. In such cases, the minutes of the relevant board meeting should record the decision and, if it is positive, also instruct and authorise the company secretary or some other suitable person to make the required, and all important, entry in the register of members. Refusal of an application would need to be based on firm and clear grounds, such as failure to meet eligibility criteria for the relevant membership category.

A membership certificate is not required by law. Some companies find it helpful to issue certificates to their members but increasingly, especially in charities with a reasonably large membership, considerations of cost and environmental protection suggest membership cards or similar, if used at all, should be one-off items (not re-issued annually on renewal of the annual membership subscription).

Entering a new member into the register of members is critical, as it is that entry which formally constitutes the applicant a legal member of that company. The entry should always be made as soon as possible after the application has been approved.

3.9.4 Admission of new members – companies limited by shares

The initial shareholders (ie the first ever members) of a company limited by shares are its subscribers, listed in the memorandum provided to Companies House as part of the incorporation process. At the moment that new company is incorporated they automatically become the members, with the shareholdings indicated against their names in the incorporation application. Their details, including the number and class of shares and the amounts paid up on each share, should be recorded in the register of members as soon as practicable. Each member is also entitled to receive a share certificate, which must be issued within 2 months.

Subsequent to incorporation, new members join the company by acquiring shares in it. There are two legal routes by which they can acquire a shareholding:

(a)   an allotment of new shares; or

(b)   a transfer of shares from an existing shareholder (the transferor) to the new member (the transferee).

Different legal rules and procedures apply to these two routes, so each is explored separately below.

3.9.5   Admittance to share company membership by allotment of shares

If the company was incorporated on or after 1 October 2009 it has no inherent limit on the number of share available to issue (ie no 'authorised share capital' level). However, an older company will have had an authorised share capital limit under previous company legislation. Such a limit remains effective, because of transitional rules for implementation of the Companies Act 2006, *unless* the company has altered its articles to remove that limit or its members have passed an ordinary resolution to remove it.

A number of other legal controls affect the allotment of additional shares. Firstly, any allotment rules in the individual company's articles will need to be checked and the relevant requirements followed. For example there may be rights of pre-emption in favour of existing shareholders, or a limit on the number of shares that can be allotted to any shareholder, or restrictions on the allotment price.

The Companies Act 2006 provides an automatic authority to the directors to allot shares (subject to the particular allotment rules in the individual company's articles) – see section 550 of the Companies Act 2006. However, this only applies if the company has a single class of ordinary shares. In a company that has two or more share classes, perhaps to reflect different types of members, the Companies Act 2006 requires the shareholders to give the directors authority to allot before an allotment of shares can be made. The authority must be given in accordance with section 551 of the Companies Act 2006. It can be specific, for a particular allotment, or general allowing shares to be allotted up to a stated maximum number for a stated period (of not more than 5 years). The authority can be given by ordinary resolution or by a clause in the articles.

The section 551 rules modify the position under previous company law (section 80 of the Companies Act 1985), which required a similar authority to be given, before any allotments could be made – even if there was only one class of ordinary shares. A company incorporated prior to 1 October 2009 remains subject to the limits of any pre-existing 'section 80' authority, so its directors are limited by the boundaries of that authority until it expires at the end of its duration or is revoked in the meantime by an ordinary resolution.

A final statutory hurdle to overcome before allotting shares is provided by sections 560–577 of the Companies Act 2006. These apply statutory pre-emption rights, requiring shares to be allotted to existing shareholders, pro rata to current holdings, if the shares to be allotted are 'equity securities'. Essentially, equity securities in this context are ordinary shares other than shares that, as respects dividend and capital, carry a right to participate only up to a specified amount in a distribution. Since most private share companies have some ordinary shares (and often *only* ordinary shares), it is important to be aware of these compulsory offer requirements.

These statutory pre-emption rights can be disapplied by special resolution or by a clause in the company's articles. The best approach, for most companies, is to ensure there is a complete disapplication by a suitable clause in the articles.

The decision to allot is most likely to rest with the board of directors. However, occasionally a company's articles will require a shareholders' resolution to make the allotment (this is unusual but certainly possible). So it is important that the right group of people take the decision and the minutes record matters accurately.

Any minute relating to a share allotment should be complete and adequate in the details recorded. Those details should include:

- the full name of the allottee;

- the date of allotment;

- the number and class of shares being allotted; and

- the terms of the allotment, in particular what is to be paid for the shares allotted, whether it is cash* (which is most common) or some other form of payment, and when that payment is to be made.

> *   Note that if shares are to be allotted for non-cash consideration, issues arise with regard to the valuation and there may be tax implications (for instance, if the assets transferred in return for the allotment give rise to a charge to stamp duty). Professional advice should be sought before embarking on an allotment for non-cash consideration.

As the decision is made to allot the shares, the directors should give the company secretary, or some other suitable person, authority to make the entry in the register of members and authorise the execution of the share certificate. The register entry is critical, as it is only when the entry is made that the share is actually issued in law and the allottee becomes a legal member of the company. Note that the share certificate is evidence of the shareholding but does not carry the ultimate legal authority of the register entry. However, a certificate must be issued within 2 months (see section 769 of the Companies Act 2006).

3.9.6 Admittance to share company membership by transfer of shares

A new member may also be admitted to a share company by means of a transfer of shares. This involves transferring the ownership, and thus both the beneficial interests and the legal title to the shares, from their current owner (ie the registered holder of those shares) to another person.

If the shares are held by a nominee, on behalf of a separate beneficial owner under a trust arrangement, a transfer will only move the legal title. Other steps would be necessary to change the beneficial ownership.

As with an allotment, the individual company's articles must be checked before embarking on a share transfer, as they may restrict how shares can be transferred. Any rules in the articles regarding transfer must be observed and the directors are responsible for ensuring this is done.

A suitable form of share transfer document needs to be completed and signed. If the shares are fully paid, only the transferor (the person getting rid of shares) needs to sign the form. However, if the shares are nil or partly paid, both transferor and transferee should do so. The transferee's signature evidences that he understands he is acquiring an asset that has an inherent financial liability (to pay the company the balance due on the shares).

Shares are property, so whilst they may be given as a gift they can also be sold to the new owner. Where that occurs, the transfer is subject to stamp duty if the consideration is more than £1,000. The company must ensure any stamp duty has been paid before the transfer is approved by the directors for registration in the register of members. Registration of an inadequately stamped transfer form renders the company secretary liable to a fine under the Stamp Act 1891.

A common source of confusion is the difference between payment to the transferor by the transferee of the price agreed on sale of shares by way of transfer and the sums paid up on the nominal value of the shares to the company. It is the former sum that dictates the rate of any stamp duty payable on a share transfer, in much the same way as the purchase price for a house sale dictates any stamp duty payable on that transaction. As with the house purchase analogy, the purchaser pays the duty.

Registration in the register of members should be authorised by the board of directors, the old share certificate must be surrendered and cancelled and a new certificate issued to the new registered holder of the shares (within 2 months, see section 776 of the Companies Act 2006). The register entry is critical, as it is only when that entry is made that the legal level of ownership passes to the new shareholder (provided it was held by the transferor, the beneficial interest passes as the transfer form is completed, so technically the outgoing shareholder is a nominee for the transferee, as the new beneficial owner, at that point).

3.10   Cessation of membership

Membership of an organisation can end by choice, for example by transfer of shares in a company limited by shares or by voluntary resignation in a guarantee company or unincorporated members' association. It can also end by 'operation of law' (as in the case of a member's death) or by some forcible termination of membership – perhaps for non-payment of an annual subscription or at the end of a disciplinary process.

3.10.1   Forcible termination of membership

The rules in the organisation's constitution need to be considered carefully and followed properly in any case of forcible termination of membership. So, for example, a member cannot be expelled unless the constitution empowers the board, or the members in general meeting, to take an expulsion decision in certain circumstances. The rules of natural justice also need to be considered, so for instance there should be a clear and fair process, involving the right for the member in question to know the basis for the proposed expulsion and to have the opportunity to put his case before any decision is made. It is not a strict legal requirement to include an appeal process, but it is good practice to do so.

Few not-for-profit companies are limited by shares. For those that are, forcible termination of membership carries added legal complications because the member owns shares. It is possible for provisions in the company's articles to force a compulsory transfer of a member's shares to someone else in specified circumstances, in order to terminate his membership. However, such provisions must be very carefully drafted and very carefully operated in practice, as there are risks that the aggrieved member may challenge an attempted compulsory transfer of his shares. Appropriate specialist legal assistance should be sought before attempting to introduce new compulsory transfer rules into a company's articles or attempting to make use of existing rules.

3.10.2 Automatic termination of membership

Some organisations include provisions in their constitutions for automatic termination of membership in specified circumstances, such as non-payment of the required annual subscription for the class of membership held. This is different from, and must not be confused with, the power to forcibly remove a member by following a particular process (see para 3.10.1).

3.10.3 Termination by operation of law

Membership of a company limited by guarantee (including a guarantee CIC) and membership of an unincorporated members' association is personal and therefore unique to the individual. This means that the member has no 'ownership' of rights that can be passed on to a successor on the member's death. His membership rights are personal to him and end by operation of law on his death.

3.10.4 Termination by resignation

Termination of membership by voluntary resignation is the most common route by which a member's membership of an organisation comes to an end. The constitution may include particular procedures that must be followed, such as a requirement for a particular period of written notice of the proposed resignation date.

In a company limited by guarantee (including a guarantee CIC) the cessation of the membership must be recorded in the register of members against the former member's entry. It is not necessary to notify Companies House.

In a company limited by shares, resignation is not an effective method of ending membership. Instead, voluntary withdrawal from membership requires a formal legal transfer of the member's shareholding to a new holder, with registration in the register of members completing the legal transfer of membership from the old to the new member.

3.11 Members' meetings

Formal meetings of the members may be held from time to time. This may occur because the constitution demands it, for instance, most membership organisations have constitutional requirements for an AGM of their members. It may also occur because there is some particular decision to be taken or authorisation needed which either the law or the constitution requires to be dealt with by the members, not by the organisation's governing body.

Examples of matters that are likely to need a members' decision or otherwise need the authority of the members are:

- a change to the organisation's name;

- alteration of the constitution;

- a decision to wind up a solvent organisation (winding up of an insolvent organisation is more likely to be triggered by legal action taken by creditors or the exercise of other rights by creditors).

Charities need prior permission from the relevant charity regulator for any change to their objects (as those are their charitable purposes). Certain other decisions and constitutional changes will also need such consent.

In some but certainly not all charities and other not-for-profits, appointments of officers and appointments of members of the governing body may be matters requiring decisions of the members (because of provisions in the individual charity's constitution).

3.11.1 Members' meetings – companies

Company law reserves a number of important matters to the members of the company, the board of directors does not have the legal capacity to deal with those things. They include any alteration of the articles and a change of name (unless the articles allow a change by some other method, which is uncommon and unlikely in a charity or not-for-profit company). The formal members' decision on such matters, known as a resolution of the members, is normally taken at a formal meeting of the members (ie at a general meeting of the company).

The requirements for arranging and holding a valid members' meeting in a company are determined by the Companies Act 2006 and related regulations made under the Act. They are also subject to the company's own articles of association, in so far as the Companies Act allows the articles to supplement the company law rules or, in some instances, to depart from a company law default rule. However, there are some company law rules relevant to members' meetings which are mandatory. These override anything in the company's articles and any contradictory article is ineffective and must be ignored on these particular points. For example, the articles cannot inhibit members' legal rights to use proxies. Considerable care must be taken to distinguish accurately between Companies Act optional and default rules and Companies Act mandatory requirements for general meetings of the members of a company.

3.11.2   Annual general meetings

An AGM is required if the organisation's constitution imposes a requirement to hold AGMs. For companies, there is no statutory requirement but any requirement imposed by the articles must be observed.

3.11.3   Annual general meeting business

The formal business of the AGM will normally be indicated in the organisation's constitution. This may include appointment of officers, such as the chairman and treasurer and a secretary, if the organisation has chosen to have one. In some but by no means all charities and other not-for-profits, some or all of the other board members, besides the principal officers, may be appointed at the AGM. This may be done through a fixed term period of office, so appointments are made if terms are ending, or through a retirement by rotation system.

For a charity, the formal AGM business typically includes presenting the annual accounts and trustees' report for the preceding financial year. If the charity is unincorporated, the accounts may need the formal approval of the membership. However, in a charitable company it is the legal responsibility of the trustees, as directors, to approve the accounts as well as their annual trustees' report (sections 414 and 419 of the Companies Act 2006). So a charitable company's members simply 'receive' the accounts and reports, there is no need for any formal approval and there should not be any resolution at the AGM purporting to give such approval.

In all charities it is appropriate that important aspects of the financial results and the impact of key activities in the past year are pointed out to members. It is also important that the members have chance to ask questions, if they wish to do so.

For further material on AGMs, see Chapter 4, para 4.9.

3.11.4   Compulsory members' meeting – Scottish charitable incorporated organisations and charitable incorporated organisations

SCIOs are legally obliged to hold a members' meeting at least every 15 months. The SCIO Regulations therefore oblige an SCIO to provide for this in its constitution.

A CIO also has an obligation to hold a regular meeting of its members (section 223(3) of the Charities Act 2011). Further detailed requirements for this can be set out in regulations.

3.12   Members' responsibilities and liabilities

Generally, members of organisations do not have significant legal responsibilities or potential liabilities in the way that the governing body's members do (as charity trustees, directors, committee members in an unincorporated members' organisation, etc). However, there may be some constitutionally based responsibilities attached to their membership by the constitution and/or supporting rules and bye-laws, for example in relation to payment of annual membership subscriptions, codes of behaviour or disciplinary matters.

Company members have responsibilities with regard to their guarantee or their shareholding, but in both those situations they also have limited liability protection.

There are some legal difficulties and uncertainties about potential liability risks for members of unincorporated members' associations.

3.12.1   Membership guarantee – guarantee companies

In a company or CIC limited by guarantee the members are subject to the 'guarantee'. This obliges them to pay a specified amount in the event of the company being wound up whilst they are members or within a year after their membership ceases (section 11 of the Companies Act 2006). The guarantee is an obligation, though it is extremely unlikely to be called upon in practice. It is also a key protection for the members against personal liability for the company's debts and other liabilities, should the company enter insolvent liquidation. The member cannot be forced to contribute towards any deficiency of funds beyond the level of his or her membership guarantee.

The guarantee sum is normally set at a nominal level, typically £1. The level of the guarantee applies equally to all the company's members (unlike membership subscription levels which can differ between different membership classes).

3.12.2 Shareholdings – share companies

In a company limited by shares, the members must pay for shares allotted to them. It is not permissible to allot shares 'at a discount' so the member is liable to pay up to the company, as a minimum, the face or 'nominal' value of shares allotted. It is possible for the member to commit to pay a further amount of share premium but this is rare in a not-for-profit share company. Usually, the member pays the nominal value per share as an immediate cash payment at the time of the allotment of the shares.

If shares remain unpaid when a company enters liquidation, the liquidator can call for payment from the shareholder. However, the shares held also act as the limited liability protection for that shareholder, as he or she cannot be required to pay more than the sum per share that he or she committed to pay the company at the date of the allotment of those shares.

3.12.3 Members' liabilities – unincorporated members' associations

The law concerning unincorporated associations is common law, rather than statute based, and is far from a comprehensive or fully satisfactory legal regime. The lack of legal personality for such associations is the underlying reason for the lack of clarity about members' liabilities (and, indeed, the liabilities of officers and committee members).

The association has no distinct legal identity so it cannot of itself enter into contracts with its own members (eg when they purchase drinks in the club bar) or with third parties (eg the drinks supplier). The member buying the drink would be most surprised if he knew that the other members of the club are releasing the value of their share in that drink to him in consideration of his payment (*Carlton Lodge Club v Customs & Excise Commissioners* [1975] 1 WLR 66 (CA)).

There is no clear legal boundary on members' liabilities to third parties. Whilst in the first instance the aggrieved party would look to the association's assets for recompense, there are potential problems about extension of liabilities to officers or even members of the association if the assets are insufficient. If the officers acted wrongly, the risk should only lie against them but if they acted properly, within the scope of their authority and with the members' approval, the aggrieved party might attempt to recover against the wider membership.

By contrast, the courts have consistently held that the management committee of an unincorporated members' association do not owe a duty of care to those members (see eg *Harrison v West of Scotland Kart Club* 2004 SC 615; *Milne v Duguid* 1999 SCLR 512; *Carmichael v Bearsden & District Rifle & Pistol Club* 2000 SLT (Sh Ct) 49; *Prole v Allen* [1950] 1 All ER 476; *Shore v Ministry of Works* [1950] 2 All ER 228; *Robertson v Ridley* [1989] 1 WLR 872 (CA)).

These unsatisfactory uncertainties, and other problems, have been highlighted by the Scottish Law Commission, which also noted that the English position gives rise to similar concerns. Its recommendations for reform suggest pan-UK change would be appropriate (see *Report on Unincorporated Associations 2009* (Scot Law Com No 217)).

3.12.4 Members' responsibilities, duties and liabilities – charitable incorporated organisations and Scottish charitable incorporated organisations

Members of CIOs and SCIOs have responsibilities specific to their class of membership in the individual organisation's articles (which may be supplemented by rules and bye-laws for detailed matters, such as annual subscription amounts).

They are also subject to a specific statutory duty of members. For a CIO's members, this duty is to exercise their powers as members in such a way as they decide, in good faith, would be most likely to further the CIO's charitable purposes (section 220 of the Charities Act 2011).

Members of an SCIO have a general duty, in exercising their membership rights, to act in the interests of the SCIO and in particular to seek, in good faith, to ensure the SCIO itself acts in a manner which is consistent with its purposes (see sections 51 and 66(1)(a), (3) and (4) of the Charities and Trustee Investment (Scotland) Act 2005).

There is no comparable statutory duty for the members of a charitable company.

Limited liability protection applies to both CIO and SCIO members. CIOs are also permitted to state in their constitutions that their members have no liability at all to contribute in the event of a winding up (as an alternative to setting a fixed nominal level of contribution) – section 206(1)(d) of the Charities Act 2011.

3.13 Membership classes

It is possible to have two or more classes of membership in a charity or not-for-profit organisation. The detail of the different rights and responsibilities of membership will be set out in the individual organisation's governing document (ie its main constitution), perhaps with supplementary detail, like levels of annual subscriptions, in subsidiary rules or bye-laws.

In the case of companies and similar corporate bodies (eg CIOs, SCIOS, CICs) the fundamental membership matters partially flow from the relevant legislation. Some of the most important rights of members cannot be removed or inhibited by provisions in the constitution, for example the right of company members to appoint proxies to attend and vote at members' general meetings on their behalf.

The Companies Act 2006 requires the rights of company members to be recorded publicly at Companies House. In share companies this is done by filing details of share classes and their rights, and information about any changes to those. For companies limited by guarantee, there are now statutory obligations to file particular forms if:

- a membership class is given a new name or its existing name is altered; and/or

- any membership class is created; and/or

- the rights of any membership class are altered.

The forms are in addition to other items that may need to be filed, such as members' resolutions and altered articles.

3.14 Members' decisions

Members' decisions may be required because of constitutional provisions or, particularly in companies, because of statutory requirements – for the members to take a particular decision or for them to authorise a particular action, event or transaction.

In some but certainly not all charities and other not-for-profits, appointments of officers and members of the governing body will be reserved by the constitution for members' decisions.

Examples of other matters that are likely to need a members' decision or otherwise need the authority of the members are:

- a change to the organisation's name;

- alteration of the constitution;

- a decision to wind up a solvent organisation (winding up of an insolvent organisation is more likely to be triggered by legal action taken by creditors or the exercise of other rights by creditors).

In an unincorporated members' association, the constitution will specify when members' decisions, rather than board decisions, are needed. It will also set out particular requirements about how the decision must be taken, such as periods of notice for a meeting or particular majorities needed to approve the proposed decision.

In a company, including a CIC, a members' decision is a formal resolution of the members. The requirement to obtain such a resolution normally arises because of specific statutory provisions in the Companies Act 2006 and/or associated regulations. The relevant provisions will specify the type of members' resolution needed for the particular matter – ordinary or special. If the requirement merely refers to 'a resolution', an ordinary resolution will suffice unless the articles require a special resolution.

The two types of members' resolution in a company are:

- *ordinary resolution* – which is passed by a 'simple majority'; and

- *special resolution* – which must be proposed as a special resolution, set out in full on the notice of meeting (if it is to be proposed at a meeting) and passed by a majority of not less than 75%.

A 'simple majority' on a vote taken *at a meeting* means:*

- on a show of hands, a simple majority of the *votes cast* by members or proxies for members;

- on a poll vote, a simple majority *of the total voting rights* of the members voting (in person or by proxy).

   *   See sections 282 and 283 of the Companies Act 2006, as amended by the Companies (Shareholders' Rights) Regulations 2009 (SI 2009/1632).

For a special resolution, where the vote is taken *at a meeting*, 'passed by a majority of not less than 75%' means:*

- on a show of hands, passed by not less than 75% of the members and proxies who vote;

- on a poll, not less than *75% of the total voting rights* of the members voting (in person or by proxy).

   *   See sections 282 and 283 of the Companies Act 2006, as amended by the Companies (Shareholders' Rights) Regulations 2009 (SI 2009/1632).

So those abstaining and non-attenders do not directly influence the outcome of the vote.

It should be noted that the calculation of the majority for a special resolution differs at a meeting than the calculation applicable if the resolution is to be passed as a written resolution. For further details on written resolutions, see para 3.14.2.

In most circumstances, a company has the option of using a members' written resolution or holding a meeting of the members to pass a members' resolution.

3.14.1   Members' decisions at general meetings (companies)

General meetings is the generic term used in the Companies Act 2006 for all formal meetings of the members of a company, including AGMs and what were once more commonly termed 'extraordinary general meetings'. The Companies Act provides a framework of rules and procedures for general meetings. In some matters, the individual company's articles can make alternative provisions.

However, some provisions of the Companies Act 2006 are mandatory. These override anything in the company's articles and any contradictory article is ineffective and must be ignored on these particular points (for example, the articles cannot inhibit members' legal rights to use proxies). Considerable care must be taken to distinguish accurately between Companies Act optional and default rules and Companies Act mandatory requirements for general meetings of the members of a company.

There must be a notice of the meeting, which must be served on all those entitled to notices of general meetings – usually all the members and also the directors (who may not be members). If the company has auditors, a copy should also be provided to them. In addition, in a share company, any person entitled to shares by reason of a member's death or bankruptcy should be given a copy (ie the personal representatives/ trustee in bankruptcy).

The notice must state the time, date and place of the meeting and the general business to be dealt with (but note that if a special resolution is to be proposed that must be specified and the full text of the resolution set out). The notice must also set out certain statements about members' rights with regard to the use of proxies.

A period of 14 clear days' notice is required (the date of the meeting and the date notice is served or deemed served are excluded). However, longer notice is required if:

- the company's articles specify a longer period;* or

- the proposed resolution relates to the forcible removal of a director or auditor.

    * This is likely in older companies, their articles often require 21 clear days' notice of a meeting to consider a special resolution.

The notice can be served in person or by post. The use of electronic communications is also possible but that is subject to the detailed provisions in the Companies Act 2006, in particular Schedule 5 (electronic communications by a company to its members).

At a meeting, a quorum must be present in order to conduct business. The relevant quorum will be set out in the articles. If they are silent, the Companies Act 2006 default rules specify two 'qualifying persons' (ie individual members or their proxies or authorised representatives or proxies of corporate members). The exception is a single member company, which may validly hold a meeting with just one person present (section 318(1) of the Companies Act 2006).

A member has an absolute right to appoint a proxy to attend a meeting on his behalf. The proxy can be anyone of the member's choice. The proxy may be instructed how to vote or authorised to make his own decision. The company's articles cannot override these rights (eg attempt to restrict the choice of proxy) and any attempt to do so is invalid.

Corporate members can attend and vote at a general meeting by appointing an authorised representative or a proxy. Following reforms introduced by the Companies Act 2006, there is little practical difference between these.

Generally, voting is conducted by show of hands. However, it can also be by poll (effectively a written ballot). The Companies Act 2006 provides minimum rights for members to demand a poll, an individual company's articles may add to those (but cannot remove or limit them).

Other rules regarding conduct of a meeting are usually set out in the articles, which should deal with matters such as chairing of the meeting, members' voting rights and the mechanics of voting, as well as potential adjustments. Again, to the extent the articles are silent there are default rules in the Companies Act 2006.

3.14.2 Members' decisions by written resolutions

An unincorporated members' association may make provision in its constitution for written resolutions of its members, as an alternative to decisions at meetings. If the constitution is silent there is no statutory alternative procedure (though probably as a matter of common law a *unanimous* decision of the members would be binding).

Whilst the articles of a company may also contain relevant provisions, the principal authority for the use of written resolutions is the Companies Act 2006 (sections 288–300). If a resolution is passed in accordance with the statutory procedure it will be valid and effective, so the safest option is to follow that procedure. However, note that a written resolution cannot be used for the removal of a director or an auditor before their period of office has ended (section 288(2) of the Companies Act 2006).

Proposed written resolutions must be sent or submitted to every 'eligible member', that is the members entitled to vote on it at the circulation date (which is the date the first member is contacted, if the copies are dispatched to different members at different times). The copies can be provided in hard copy form or by electronic communication (subject to the specific rules on such communication from a company to its members in the Companies Act 2006).

If the proposed written resolution is a special resolution, that must be clearly stated in the circulated resolution.

Any auditors in office have the right to receive all communications that members receive regarding written resolutions (section 502(1) of the Companies Act 2006).

The period allowed for indications of agreement to the resolution by the required percentage of the eligible members is 28 days, beginning with the circulation date (or an alternative period specified in the company's articles). If the necessary consents are not received within that period, the resolution will lapse.

A member can give his consent by hard copy or, provided the company is willing to accept it, by electronic form. Note that electronic communications to a company by an individual member must comply with the requirements of Schedule 4 to the Companies Act 2006, whereas communications by a company (eg from a corporate member to the company) must comply with the provisions of Schedule 5, which are not identical. Both Schedules apply regardless of anything in the company's articles.

The percentage consent required to pass a written resolution is:

- for an ordinary resolution, a simple majority of the total voting rights of the eligible members;

- for a special resolution, a majority of not less than 75% of the total voting rights of the eligible members.

There are requirements to keep a record of written resolutions and these must be retained for at least 10 years. Where any such record is signed by a director or the secretary, it provides evidence of the passing of the resolution. It is also deemed that the requirements in the Companies Act 2006 with regard to the passing of written resolutions were complied with (see section 355(1)(a) and (2) and section 356(2) and (3) of the Companies Act 2006).

4 Constitutions and Legal Administration

4.1 Introduction

The constitution of an organisation is its governing document. It sets the framework for the governance of that organisation and provides the internal rules for its administration. It does so in the legal context of:

- the rules applicable to the organisation because of its particular legal form (eg company, CIO or SCIO, CIC);

- the obligations that arise because of the special legal nature of the organisation's purposes and activities (eg if those are charitable).

An organisation must be governed and operated in accordance with its own constitution (save where the law imposes any overriding requirement – eg compulsory time limits for filing data and documents with regulators). The constitution is of fundamental importance, so board members should ensure they and senior staff, officers and key volunteers are familiar with it.

It is an inherent part of the duties of charity trustees and company directors to ensure their charity or company does not go beyond the limitations in its own constitution and otherwise operates in accordance with it. Failure to do so could lead to personal liabilities for breach of duty and, in the case of a charity, perhaps for breach of trust.

It is essential that anyone accessing the constitution is aware of all amendments to date. Whilst the constitution may still be the original founding document, unaltered, it may be that there have been subsequent alterations or it may have been replaced entirely by a new constitution. If an unincorporated organisation incorporates (eg as a company limited by guarantee), a new and different corporate body comes into being, with its own constitution (articles of association, in the case of a company).

4.2   The legal form of the constitution

The legal form of the constitution will be dictated by the legal form of the organisation.

Type of organisation	Type of constitution
Company (limited by shares or by guarantee)	Articles of association (memorandum and articles, for companies incorporated before 1 October 2009)
Community interest company	Articles of association (memorandum and articles, for companies incorporated before 1 October 2009)
Body incorporated by Royal Charter	Royal Charter (and rules and bye-laws made pursuant to that charter, these are subsidiary to the charter itself)
Charitable incorporated organisation/Scottish charitable incorporated organisation	Constitution
Unincorporated trust	Trust deed or trust document (sometimes a declaration of trust will have been made within another document, eg a will)
Unincorporated members' association	Constitution or rules
Industrial and provident society	Rules
Statutory corporation (eg National Trust and some health service charities)	Relevant Act of Parliament/ regulations will specify the constitutional requirements

Note that the legal rules relevant to the trust deed of an unincorporated trust and the constitutions of an unincorporated members' association are largely common law based, rather than statutory as is the case for companies, CICs, CIOs and SCIOs.

4.3   Constitutions of charities – general matters

The constitution of a charity will contain certain key elements because of the charitable status. In particular:

*   the charitable purposes (or 'objects');

*   provisions requiring the charity's funds and assets to be applied to those purposes;

*   bans or restrictions on any benefits to the trustees and, if it is a membership charity, also limits on benefits to the members;

*   a requirement for any surplus funds on winding up to be transferred to a charity with similar charitable purposes.

Generally, there will also be provisions regarding the appointment of trustees, powers for the charity to use in furthering its charitable purposes (exercisable by the board) and some specific powers of the board.

A charity constitution should comply with charity law and with legal provisions relevant to the particular legal form chosen for that charity, for example company law in the case of a charitable company limited by guarantee. Note there are specific statutory rules concerning the required contents of constitutions for CIOs and SCIOs.

Care must be taken to interpret the effect of provisions in constitutions correctly against the wider law. Some legal rules are mandatory, so any contradictory provision in an individual charity's constitution would be ineffective in those instances. Other rules are default rules, applying if the constitution does not contain alternative provisions. For example a charitable company's articles can impose a requirement for the holding of an AGM or the appointment of a secretary, which would otherwise not be required under the Companies Act 2006 rules for private companies. If the individual charitable company's articles do this, those provisions override the statutory default position and the articles must be obeyed.

In any charity, a specific constitutional obligation to appoint auditors and have the annual accounts audited must be observed. The audit exemption options provided by the law do not override that obligation.

However, on fundamental charity law matters, the wider law, not the constitution, will normally prevail. For example, a provision of the constitution cannot remove fundamental charity law protections of the charitable assets or authorise misuse of those assets for non-charitable purposes.

4.4   Companies incorporated under the Companies Act 2006

A company incorporated under the Companies Act 2006 (on or after 5 October 2009) has a single constitutional document – articles of association. This includes all relevant external matters, such as the limited liability clause, as well as the internal rules for the company's operation and management. For a guarantee company, the limited liability clause includes a fixed level guarantee for each member (typically a nominal figure, eg £1). This is crucial, as it caps the level of each member's potential personal liability to contribute to the company's debts and other liabilities in the event of a winding up.

A company incorporated under the Companies Act 2006 does not need to specify objects to meet company law requirements for incorporation. Its objects are unrestricted unless the articles set out specific restrictions (section 31 of the Companies Act 2006).

So company law starts from the premise that a new company is free to carry on any lawful business activities, at the discretion of its board. Clearly this is a positive aspect of the new law for trading subsidiaries but not appropriate for many not-for-profits such as clubs and associations. It is untenable for a charity because a charity must have purely charitable purposes, with no non-charitable element. The charity regulators therefore expect a clear, short provision setting out the charitable purposes in the articles. In this context, note the different lists of potentially charitable purposes set out in the relevant legislation of England and Wales, Scotland and Northern Ireland (for details, see Chapter 1).

The articles will also contain key internal rules regarding governance and administration of the company. Areas of particular importance are trustees and the operation of the board (eg how trustees take decisions), members and membership rights and responsibilities.

The Companies Act 2006 also includes certain other documents, besides the articles, in the legal concept of a company's 'constitution'. These are any resolutions or agreements affecting the articles that are covered by section 29 of the Act (see also section 17).

There are Companies Act 2006 rules regarding 'provision for entrenchment' in a company's articles and requirements to give notice to the registrar about such provisions in certain circumstances (sections 22–24 of the Companies Act 2006). Entrenched provisions in articles are unusual.

4.4.1 Chairman's casting vote

It is no longer possible for a company's articles to give a casting vote to the chairman of a general meeting of the company's members (though this can still be done for a chairman at a board meeting). This is because of the wording of the Companies Act 2006 with regard to voting at general meetings (sections 281 and 282 of the Companies Act 2006).

Transitional provisions allow a casting vote for the chairman in these situations:

(a)   if there is provision for it in articles and that provision was in force prior to 1 October 2007; or

(b)   there used to be such a provision, it was removed by a change to the articles made on or after 1 October 2007 but the provision has subsequently been reinstated.

4.4.2 Constitutions of community interest companies

The constitution of a CIC is its articles of association – remember that CICs are a type of company. The legal requirements for a CIC's articles flow from the Companies Act 2006 but also the specific CIC legislation, in particular the relevant regulations (the Community Interest Regulations 2005 (SI 2005/1788) as amended by the Companies Act 2006 (Commencement No 2, Consequential Amendments, Transitional Provisions and Savings) Order 2007 (SI 2007/1093)). The collective effect is more prescriptive than company law is in relation to the articles of other companies, so particular care needs to be taken in preparing a CIC constitution to observe the legal restrictions.

The objects of a CIC need to be specifically set out and must meet the 'community interest test'. For further details, see Chapter 1.

The 'asset lock' rules affect the provisions of a CIC's articles. They must ensure that transfers of assets at less than market value are only permitted to other specified asset locked bodies. If the articles deal with the application of final funds in the event of a winding up, they must require the transfer to be to particular asset locked bodies with similar community benefit purposes to the CIC itself. If not, the CIC Regulator has the power to direct which body or bodies will take custody of those final funds.

An asset locked body is:

- another CIC;

- a UK charity;

- equivalents to either of the above established outside the UK.

See regulation 2 of the Community Interest Regulations 2005 (as amended by the Companies Act 2006 (Commencement No 2, Consequential Amendments, Transitional Provisions and Savings) Order 2007).

In addition, the CIC's articles need to comply with the legal controls and restrictions on the funding of CICs (in relation to their borrowings and limits on interest payment arrangements), limitations on dividends for dividend bearing shares (for CICs limited by shares) and controls on payments and benefits to directors. There is a certain amount of flexibility but that is set within specific parameters which need to be observed with care when drafting or altering articles.

There are model forms of articles for the different types of CIC (private limited by shares, private limited by guarantee, etc). Whilst those are not strictly compulsory, the law requires CIC articles to include particular features. These relate to limits on dividend payments (share CICs) and certain performance-related interest payments to lenders, restrictions on transfers of assets at less than full value (save to other named asset locked bodies).

The above comments relate to CICs incorporated under the Companies Act 2006 on or after 1 October 2009. Older CICs will have a double constitution (memorandum and articles) created under the previous legal requirements. The memorandum is now deemed part of the articles, as is the case for other older companies.

4.5   Companies incorporated before 1 October 2009

The Companies Act 1985 required a company to have a memorandum of association and separate articles of association. These were normally bound together in one document and referred to as the memorandum and articles of association, but they were in fact legally two different documents.

The memorandum dealt with matters external to the company and was required to contain:

- the company's name (ie the name taken at the date of incorporation);

- the jurisdiction of registration (England and Wales, Scotland, Northern Ireland);

- the company's objects;

- the limitation of liability clause (if the company was a limited company);

- the authorised share capital clause for companies limited by shares (this gave details of the class, number and nominal value of the original shares, as at the date of incorporation) *or* the guarantee clause for companies limited by guarantee.

The objects were either set out in full, listing activities linked to the main purpose or principal business activities, or the 'general commercial company object' could be used. This permitted the company to carry on any trade or business and do anything incidental or conducive to carrying on any business. That was often helpful in a trading subsidiary, so business activities could be altered from time to time without delay and the administrative and legal formalities of a formal change to the memorandum. Charities and other specialist companies, such as CICs, did not use the general commercial company clause but would set out short and very specific objects, limiting their activities to the relevant charitable or community benefit purposes.

Some of the provisions in the memorandum were largely of historic interest, others were fixed once and for all (eg a company registered in one part of the UK cannot migrate its registration to another jurisdiction) whilst others operated as limitations on the company (eg the authorised share capital level, in a company limited by shares). The objects and powers (the latter usually being set out in the objects clause) were capable of alteration by special resolution of the members of the company.

The articles were more inward facing, concerned with issues such as eligibility for membership, membership classes and members' rights, eligibility to serve as directors, the methods by which directors were appointed and how directors would cease to hold office, the calling and conduct of meetings of the board and the members and so forth. The articles could be altered by special resolution of the members of the company.

A similar regime applied to CICs, with additional restrictions and requirements regarding the contents of the memorandum and articles (eg the 'asset lock' and limits on permissible benefits to directors and, for share CICs, the level of dividends that could be paid to their shareholders).

4.5.1   Tables A and C

Successive Companies Acts, or regulations made to support them, have prescribed certain models of memoranda or articles for particular types of company (eg under the Companies Act 1985, Table A for private companies limited by shares and Table C for companies limited by guarantee). In some cases the model applied automatically to the extent the company in question did not amend or disapply all or part of it. Once applicable to a particular company, a relevant model (or the selected provisions from it) remained part of the articles, even when subsequent versions came into force. This remained the case unless and until the company altered its articles in such a way as to adopt the latest model.

It became common practice in non-charitable companies (and in many charitable companies in Scotland) to make use of much of the share company model articles – Table A – with adaptations and the removal of share-specific clauses. Many companies in the third sector have articles of association constructed in this way. Care needs to be taken in reading and applying those articles now, because:

- there have been many different versions of Table A – it is important to identify exactly which one the articles refer to;

- Table A differs significantly from the Companies Act 2006 successor 'model articles';

- Table A in all its versions no longer sits well with the very different provisions of the Companies Act 2006 (in some cases the new Act overrides on particular points but in others it does not).

4.5.2   Impact of Companies Act 2006 changes on older companies – general

As described above, the Companies Act 2006 no longer requires a separate memorandum of association as part of the constitution of new companies incorporated on or after 1 October 2009. However, it has retained the effectiveness of the memorandum of association as part of the constitution of an older company, by treating the memorandum as part of the company's articles (section 28 of the Companies Act 2006).

Full style objects therefore remain effective to place ultimate limits on what activities the company may conduct. A company with the old style 'general commercial company' object remains free to carry out any lawful business activities. Any change to either style of objects still requires a special resolution of the members. For charitable companies and CICs, the prior consent of the Charity Commission and/or the OSCR, or the CIC Regulator, must still be obtained before changing objects.

The old style articles also remain effective and, again, may still be altered by special resolution of the members.

For share companies, their authorised capital in existence on 1 October 2009 remains an effective limit on the number of shares available to issue. Remember the level of that capital may not necessarily be as set out in the memorandum of association, since there may have been alterations by share capital increases since incorporation. This limit of the current level as at 1 October 2009 can be removed by resolution of the members.

Likewise, any authority for the directors of a share company to allot shares (given under section 80 of the Companies Act 1985) remains effective as a limit on the directors' freedom to make further allotments. That authority may still relate to a clause in the old style articles or it may relate to an ordinary resolution of the members passed under the relevant provisions of the old law. This 'carried forward' limitation can also be removed by a resolution of the company's members.

4.5.3   Companies Act 2006 – the old 'Tables'

The Companies Act 2006 has abolished the old statutory models of articles (the various 'Tables') for *new* share companies and *new* guarantee companies. Older companies are still subject to any relevant Table applicable as part of their articles (the new model articles do not automatically apply to them). A company can choose to update its articles in full and make use of all, or parts of, the relevant new model (or to disapply the entirety of that model, if preferred). This would require a special resolution of the company's members.

4.6   Constitutions of charitable incorporated organisations and Scottish charitable incorporated organisations

The legal requirements for the constitutions of CIOs and SCIOs are partially determined by the principal legislation (the Charities Act 2006 and the Charities and Trustee Investment (Scotland) Act 2005 respectively). However, further detail is added by separate regulations in each jurisdiction.

4.7   Altering constitutions

Constitutions need to change and evolve. Drivers for change may include:

- expansion or contraction of the organisation (eg in membership, operations and activities, geographical 'reach', financial scale);

- changes to the needs of beneficiaries and/or new needs or new ways of meeting them (charities) or changes to the relevant community and its needs (CICs);

- funding pressures and changes;

- external pressures and changes (eg in wider society);

- strategic planning and review by the board;

- a constitutional review or 'health check';

- mergers or other forms of restructuring;

- concerns of a regulator (eg that the organisation is going beyond its purposes or failing to deliver adequate charitable public benefit (charity) or community benefit in accordance with the 'community interest test' (CIC));

- legal changes (eg in charity or company law).

4.7.1   Regulatory consents

Sometimes the organisation must obtain prior consent from a relevant regulator before it can make proposed changes to its constitution. The principal circumstances in which this arises are summarised below. Changes to charity constitutions made without appropriate consent will be ineffective.

Charitable companies in England and Wales must obtain prior Charity Commission consents for these 'regulated alterations' (section 198(2) of the Charities Act 2011):

- altering the charitable purposes (objects) (by alteration, addition or removal of wording);

- altering anything which directs how the charitable company's property is to be applied on the company's dissolution;

- altering to provide authorisation of any benefit to be obtained by trustees or members of the company or persons connected with them.

For charities on the Scottish Charity Register, the prior consent of the OSCR is necessary for any alteration of the charitable purposes (section 16 of the Charities and Trustee Investment (Scotland) Act 2005). The consent must be applied for at least 42 days before it is intended to be made, so adequate forward planning is essential.

For CICs, the prior consent of the CIC Regulator is needed to changes of name and to certain other changes, such as alterations to the community benefit purposes or to the restrictions and controls in its articles on the application of the CIC's assets. Consent is also needed to change the CIC's status to another legal status (eg a charity).

4.7.2   Making changes – companies and community interest companies

Subject to any regulatory consent requirements, a company or CIC makes changes to its articles (or memorandum and articles for older companies) by passing a special resolution of its members. This may be done at a general meeting of the members, including but not limited to, the AGM, or by a statutory members' written resolution (sections 288–300 of the Companies Act 2006). If the latter is used, care must be taken to comply with the procedures required by the Companies Act 2006, in particular with regard to providing a copy to the auditors, determining who are the 'eligible members' who can sign the resolution, calculating the percentage required for it to be passed and determining the date on which it becomes effective. Note also the filing obligations (see para 4.7.7).

An alteration to the objects of a company does not take effect until the Registrar of Companies has registered the required documents on the company's public record (section 31(2)(c) of the Companies Act 2006).

4.7.3   Making changes – charitable incorporated organisations and Scottish charitable incorporated organisations

A similar range of 'regulated alterations' as those that apply to charitable companies apply to CIOs. Certain other proposed changes (eg amalgamation with other CIOs) must be notified to the Charity Commission. The Commission has various special powers which it may then choose to exercise (such as refusing the proposals in certain circumstances). The SCIO regulations include similar but not identical safeguards.

4.7.4   Making changes – unincorporated charitable trusts

Generally, there will be a power of amendment in the original trust document. This is likely to allow the trustees to make changes but will be subject to any requirements to obtain prior consent from relevant regulators, particularly in the case of a charitable trust. If the trust document does *not* provide a suitable power of amendment, it is likely the changes can be made under the Charities Act 2011 provisions (see para 4.7.6).

4.7.5   Making changes – unincorporated members' associations

Power to make changes to the constitution of an unincorporated members' association depends in the first instance on whether its constitution contains a power of amendment. If it does, that power is likely to require a resolution of the members and may impose particular formalities, such as notice period or majority required to approve changes.

In the case of a charity in this legal form, use of such a power will be subject to any required prior consents from relevant charity regulators. If the constitution does not provide a suitable power of amendment, it is likely the changes can be made under the Charities Act 2011 provisions (see para 4.7.6).

4.7.6   Charities Act 2011 provisions – unincorporated charities (England and Wales)

If there is no specific power of amendment in the constitution of an unincorporated registered charity, it may be possible for the trustees to use one of two statutory powers in the Charities Act 2011. However, it should be noted that these provisions cannot be used if the charity holds land given to it for its charitable purposes (or part of them).

The two statutory powers are:

- power for the trustees of a small unincorporated charity to alter its purposes (this applies only if the annual income is under £10,000, section 275 of the Charities Act 2011);

- power for the trustees of an unincorporated charity to alter provisions relating to their administrative powers and procedures (there is no income threshold on this power, section 280 of the Charities Act 2011).

To make use of the first of these two statutory powers, the trustees must be satisfied that:

- it is expedient in the interests of the charity for its current purposes to be replaced; and

- so far as reasonably practicable, the proposed new purposes are similar to those they will replace.

The trustees may resolve to use the first statutory power but if the charity has a membership (for instance, it is an unincorporated members' association, rather than a charitable trust) the members must also approve the proposed changes by resolution with a two-thirds majority in favour (or without a vote if there is no dissension).

The trustees then need to provide a copy of their decision, plus the members' decision in the case of an unincorporated members' association, to the Charity Commission, with a statement providing their reasons for making that decision. The Commission has the power to require the proposals to be advertised and it can block the change if it does not consider it to be appropriate. Subject to those two possibilities, the resolution takes effect 60 days after the copy is supplied to the Commission.

The second statutory power, to alter administrative provisions in the constitution, might, for example, be used to alter the quorum for trustees' meetings to a more practical number. Such a change is immediately effective but must be notified to the Charity Commission.

Because of these two very helpful statutory powers, it is now much rarer to have to obtain advance authority from the Charity Commission to make changes to the constitution of an unincorporated charity. However, its consent will still be needed in some cases (eg a change of objects in a charity above the £10,000 income level). In addition, there will also still be occasions when special factors, such as land subject to trusts or other endowment issues, make the process of change more legally complex. It may then be necessary to obtain a formal order or scheme to effect the required changes. Specialist professional advice should be taken in all such cases before approaching the Charity Commission.

4.7.7   Filing obligations – alteration of a company's articles

When a company makes changes to its articles (which now include the memorandum of association of a company incorporated prior to 5 October 2009), it must file these items at Companies House within 15 days of the date of the alteration:

- the special resolution that made the changes;

- a copy of the articles as altered (this should include the memorandum, with the exception of the list of subscribers, as that memorandum is now part of the articles);

- any statutory forms required in consequence of the change (eg because there have been changes to the objects or to membership classes or share class rights);

- appropriate consents to the changes from relevant regulators (eg the Charity Commission, the OSCR or the CIC Regulator).

Because a change of objects only takes effect when it is actually *registered* on the company's public record by the Registrar of Companies (section 31(2)(c) of the Companies Act 2006), it is advisable to search the register to ascertain the exact date on which the changes take legal effect.

If the company fails to send to the Registrar of Companies a copy of its altered articles within 15 days after the amendment, the Registrar may give notice to the company requiring it to comply with the filing obligation. If it still fails to do so within 28 days, an automatic civil penalty of £200 applies (see section 27 of the Companies Act 2006).

These obligations also apply to CICs which are subject to company law general filing requirements.

4.7.8   Notifying other regulators of changes

For changes where Charity Commission advance consent was needed, certified copies of the relevant resolution or document that made the agreed changes, plus a copy of the altered constitution should be provided to the Commission as soon as practicable after the date of the change. Whilst there is no specific legal requirement to do so, it is good practice to notify the Commission of all other changes.

In Scotland, it is a legal obligation to notify the OSCR of all changes to charity constitutions within 3 months (whether or not the changes required prior consent from the OSCR) (section 17 of the Charities and Trustee Investment (Scotland) Act 2005).

4.8 Legal administration

The precise requirements for the legal administration of a charity or other not-for-profit organisation will depend on its legal form, specific legislative requirements for that legal form, any special legal status it has (eg charitable status) and the specific legislative requirements that flow from that status. It will also in part be affected by the provisions of the individual organisation's constitution.

All charities and not-for-profit organisations must also comply with the legal administrative requirements of the general law in areas such as employment, insurance, tax and VAT, health and safety, data protection and much else. This has particular importance in the context of record keeping.

4.9 Annual and other general meetings

A 'general meeting' is a formal meeting of the legal members of an organisation, so the concept is only relevant to those legal forms of charities and not-for-profits that have a formal membership. Detailed rules about such meetings are normally set out in the organisation's constitution.

Companies also need to comply with the requirements of the Companies Act 2006 and in some instances those override the company's own articles (eg as to the rights of members to appoint proxies). Particular care should be taken with regard to company articles that pre-date the present Companies Act rules as they are almost certain to contain conflicting provisions, some of which will no longer have legal effect and cannot be relied on.

4.9.1 Annual general meetings – companies

Under the Companies Act 2006, there is no requirement for private companies (including charitable companies) to hold AGMs, although they may opt to do so. However, companies still need to comply with their own articles, so any requirement in the articles to hold an AGM remains effective and binding. It is very likely that any charitable company registered prior to 1 October 2007 will have a requirement for AGMs in its articles (and many other not-for-profit companies will also have such a requirement).

The liberalising provisions of the Companies Act 2006 can be particularly useful for trading subsidiary companies. However, a charity is likely to want to hold AGMs, particularly if it has a wide membership, beyond the composition of its trustee board. To do so can be a valuable part of its strategy for maintaining and developing support from its members and other stakeholders and in demonstrating the transparency and accountability appropriate to a charity.

4.9.2 Annual general meetings – other organisations

CIOs and SCIOs have a statutory obligation to hold periodic general meetings of their members.

For other legal forms of membership organisation, whether or not an AGM is an obligation and, if so, what the business of such a meeting would be, depends on the particular organisation's own constitution.

Unincorporated charitable trusts do not have such an obligation, as they do not have a formal membership.

4.9.3 Annual general meetings – date

The date requirements for AGMs will usually be specified in the constitution. It is common for the requirement to be to hold an AGM within 18 months of incorporation and for further AGMs to be held annually (in each calendar year). Usually, no more than 15 months can elapse between each AGM.

For charitable companies, because the AGM is no longer obligatory, their articles can include AGM date rules that suit their individual circumstances. It is wise to avoid being over-prescriptive and too inflexible though, so the company can select a date in each year that allows it to deal comfortably with the administrative and practical arrangements for the meeting. In addition, the Companies Act 2006 requires the annual reports and accounts to be filed at Companies House within 9 months of the financial year end. Although the members do not need to approve the accounts and reports (the board must do so), this deadline will generally influence the timing of the meeting, as these items are normally presented to the members at that meeting.

4.9.4 Annual general meetings – business

The formal business of the AGM will normally be indicated in the organisation's constitution. For further comment, see Chapter 3.

4.9.5 Extraordinary general meetings

General meetings other than the AGM are often called 'extraordinary general meetings'. The need to hold a general meeting apart from the AGM usually arises because there is a proposed change or a proposed transaction which requires a formal decision of the members or their formal permission; the board is not empowered to proceed by its own decision. In unincorporated organisations, the constitution will specify such matters.

In companies, the Companies Act 2006 imposes a range of requirements for members' resolutions rather than directors' decisions in particular situations. If it is not convenient or possible to wait until the AGM to deal with such a formal decision of the company's members, an extraordinary general meeting may be held to deal with it.

4.9.6 Meetings – chairing and conduct

The constitution of the organisation normally indicates who takes the chair at a general meeting of the members and provides some powers for the chairman of that meeting. Typically, the current chairman of the board is entitled to take the chair if attending the meeting.

The essential role of the chairman of the meeting is to ensure it is conducted in an orderly fashion and the business is properly dealt with. In addition to any specific provisions in the individual organisation's constitution about the role of the chairman, there are general legal principles for guidance, such as the need to deal fairly with all members, ensuring their rights are respected and can be exercised effectively (eg voting rights). In a company, the chairman must ensure Companies Act 2006 rules relevant to the meeting and members' resolutions are observed.

4.9.7 Meetings – quorum

The quorum is the minimum number of participants with voting rights who must be present before the meeting can validly conduct business. This is normally specified in the organisation's constitution. In the case of a company, if its articles are deficient, failing to state a quorum, the Companies Act 2006 default rule is two qualifying persons (section 318). A 'qualifying person' is:

- an individual who is a member of the company;

- an authorised representative of a corporation that is a member;

- a proxy for any member.

There is a special rule for single member companies, which can have a valid quorum of one whilst they have just one member (regardless of their articles). A charitable or not-for-profit company is unlikely to be a single member company.

4.10   Registers and records

Whilst unincorporated members' associations will normally keep some form of membership records (and are strongly advised to do so, for obvious reasons), there are no statutory requirements about the form and content of those records. The individual organisation's constitution may include some specific requirements and, if it does, they should be followed. Other records may be necessary because of general legal provisions, such as health and safety or employment legislation.

4.10.1   Statutory registers – companies

A private company must keep statutory registers that comply with company law requirements (which have been considerably altered by the Companies Act 2006). These legal requirements apply equally to charitable companies and the trading subsidiaries of charities as well as CICs and not-for-profit companies.

Registers can be kept in paper form in bound books or loose-leaf formats. Computer systems may also be used provided they can be reproduced in legible form. Whatever methods are chosen, the company must take adequate security steps to prevent and detect falsification or accidental loss or damage.

4.10.2   Register of members – companies

For each member, the details required are name, home address and dates of admission and cessation of membership. With the exception of the initial subscribers on incorporation, the only persons who are members of the company are those who have agreed to be members and whose names have been entered in the register of members. Accordingly, this register can be crucial if doubts arise over who the members are.

It is essential that the register of members is accurate and up to date. The register will need to be consulted for the proper corporate administration of the charity, for example in verifying who is entitled to attend and vote at any annual or other general meeting.

A company must be careful to record in its register of members all those who are its members for the purposes of company law. However, other persons associated with the company but not members in law (eg 'supporters' or 'associates' or directors/trustees who are not legal members) should not be recorded in this register. Separate records should be kept for such groups of people.

4.10.3 Registers of directors and secretary – companies

For directors, their name, an address, date of birth and business occupation must be specified, plus dates of appointment to and cessation of office. The address can be either their home address or a 'service address'. The service address can be simply stated as 'the registered office'.

Details of 'other directorships' are not required, but the director must give any name(s) by which he or she is, or was, known for business purposes. There is no longer an exception for a married woman's former name. The Companies Act 2006 requires a director's usual country or state of residence, or the part of the UK in which he or she is usually resident, to be recorded.

For any secretary, a name, an address and dates of appointment and cessation of office must be recorded. Again, the address can be either his or her home address or a 'service address'.

4.10.4 Register of Directors' Residential Addresses – companies

To support the rights of privacy for individual directors' residential addresses, companies must keep records of individual directors' residential addresses in the Register of Directors' Residential Addresses (RODRA). This is not open to general public access.

If the director has already entered his residential address as his service address in the Register of Directors, the RODRA need only state that fact. The exception is if the director's residential address is the registered office address, and the address given as the service address is 'the company's registered office'. In that case, the address must be given in full in the RODRA.

4.10.5 Register of charges

This must contain details of all charges that are subject to registration requirements.

4.10.6 Service addresses for members, directors, secretary – companies

The 'service address' rules came into force on 1 October 2009. A service address for an individual director can be recorded in the public part of the register, with the residential address kept separately in the RODRA. A range of regulatory and investigatory agencies can access the RODRA but it is not open to general public inspection.

The following are deemed 'protected information' by the Companies Act 2006:

(a)   that the service and residential addresses are different; or

(b)   that they are the same.

This information remains protected information even after a director has ceased to hold office, so that references to a director include a former director.

Note that the residential address must still be supplied to the Registrar of Companies. It is kept securely, with access only available to relevant authorities and credit reference agencies. The Registrar of Companies is, however, only required to protect residential addresses given officially and correctly. The Registrar is under no obligation to check that a residential address has not been given inadvertently, for example in the presenter's details on a statutory form.

A third party may want to know a director's residential address (either that a separate residential address has been given, or that the service address given is also the director's residential address). The circumstances in which this protected information may be disclosed (or used) by Companies House are:

1.   To communicate with the director.

2.   To a public authority specified in regulations.

3.   To a credit reference agency (as defined in the Consumer Credit Act 1974).

4.   If a director consents to disclosure.

The secretary of state has made regulations setting out conditions that must be satisfied before such a disclosure may be made (the Companies (Disclosure of Address) Regulations 2009 (SI 2009/214)). These include reassurances about the security measures the agency has in place to protect the data and declarations about the purposes for which it is being sought.

The regulations also set out the circumstances in which application can be made to prevent disclosure to a credit reference agency. Essentially, there must be risk of serous violence against the director or someone in his household in order to gain this added protection.

If a service address is ineffective, the Registrar of Companies can put the residential address on the public record, provided that he has sent a warning notice to the director and every company of which he or she is director. The notice must be sent to the residential address unless it appears to the Registrar that service there may be ineffective to bring it to the director's attention, in which case he can use the service address. The notice must specify the grounds upon which the Registrar proposes to put the residential address on the public record, and the period during which the director may make representations as to why his or her residential address should not be disclosed. If the director makes representations, the Registrar must consider them.

If the Registrar decides to put the residential address on the public record, he updates the public record as if he had been notified that the service address is the director's home address. The Registrar must then notify the director, and the company. The company must amend its statutory registers to include the director's residential address. If the director has notified the company of a more recent residential address, it must enter that address in its registers, and file change of particulars with the Registrar. The director is then prohibited from using a service address that is not his or her residential address for the next 5 years.

4.10.7 Location and inspection of statutory registers – companies

The default position is that a company must keep its registers available for inspection at its registered office. However, regulations made under the Companies Act 2006 allow a company to specify a single alternative inspection location (SAIL), as an alternative to the registered office, where it may keep all or any of its public records available for inspection.

The conditions that must be met in order to use a SAIL are:

1. The SAIL is situated in the part of the UK in which the company is registered.

2. The company notifies Companies House of that SAIL (form AD02).

3. The company notifies Companies House which records are kept at the SAIL (form AD03).

All records of a given type must be kept together, either at a SAIL or the registered office, they cannot be split between two locations.

A company must, within 5 working days, disclose the address of its registered office, and any address where it keeps company records available for public inspection (and the type of company records kept there), to any person it deals with in the course of its business who makes a written request to the company for that information. It must also state the SAIL address (if any), and which records are kept at the SAIL as at the return date.

The regulations require a person wishing to inspect the company's records to give the company advance notice. The notice period is generally 10 days, but is 2 days in certain specified circumstances. The records must be available for inspection on any working day for at least 2 hours between 9am and 3pm.

Changes to the rules on access to and inspection of the register of members, introduced by the Companies Act 2006, retain the general principle of public access to the register of members but also provide safeguards against potential abuses of the access right. The following rules apply:

- an access request must provide the name and address of the person making it;

- the request must say what the information will be used for, whether it will be shared with anyone else and, if so, who and for what purpose.

The company has 5 days to comply with the request (or seek a court order that the request is not made for a proper purpose). The Companies Act 2006 leaves decisions about what would or would not be a proper purpose to the courts, where any application to refuse an access request is made.

4.10.8 Non-statutory registers – companies

Most companies also keep non-statutory registers, they are usually:

- *registers of sealings and executions* – recording each use of the company seal on documents and all executions of items without the seal. Details should include the type and date of document, the parties and the names of directors/trustees who countersigned the seal or executed without the seal on the company's behalf;

- *a register of allotments (share companies)* – recording details of all share allotments;

- *a register of transfers (share companies)* – recording details of all share transfers (including transmission of shares on death or bankruptcy of a member).

4.10.9 Minutes of meetings

Charities should always keep records of formal meetings, both trustees' meetings and meetings of their members, such as the AGM. These are usually kept as minutes. Any company, including a CIC, is obliged to keep such records by Companies Act 2006 requirements. These records must be kept for a minimum of 10 years (indefinitely for minutes of meetings held before 1 October 2008).

Records of general meetings of the members of a company must be kept at the registered office and can be inspected by any member as well as any director and the company's auditor (if it has an auditor).

Board meeting minutes can be kept wherever the board deems appropriate but are only available for inspection by members of the board and the auditors. Members have no statutory right of access.

Minutes should be:

- accurate;
- brief; and
- complete.

They should also be principally minutes of record – a formal legal record of decisions taken by the relevant meeting. Sometimes, minutes of narration will be appropriate, for example the principal elements of a discussion which preceded a complex, difficult or particularly important decision or the board's reasons for determining a particular course of action (such as financial evidence of the need for or consequences of that action). Any document cross-referred to in the minutes should always be retained with them in original or copy form as appropriate (eg a budget/cash flow forecast/or a document authorised to be sealed or executed).

If a company's minutes of board or members' meetings are 'authenticated' by the chairman of the meeting in question (or the chairman of the next meeting) they are *prima facie* evidence of the matters they record. The Companies Act 2006 permits electronic authentication methods and also allows traditional signature of a hard copy.

Organisations should ensure that the authorisation procedures, access facilities (including remote electronic access) and the storage arrangements they choose in relation to minutes are appropriate and adequate (in relation to accidental loss and damage, falsification, unauthorised access, etc).

4.11 Disclosure obligations

Disclosure obligations exist for charities and companies as part of the *quid pro quo* for the benefits they enjoy through their special legal status (such as charity tax exemptions and the protection of limited liability for the members of companies). There is a valid public interest to be served by ensuring third parties are aware they are dealing with a charity or a company and by ensuring they can identify that entity correctly and establish certain key legal information about it. This is also part of the overall public accountability regime, for more information, see Chapter 5.

4.11.1 Charity disclosure obligations – England and Wales

All charities registered in England and Wales that have incomes exceeding £10,000 must state that they are a registered charity on the items listed below:

- notices, advertisements or other documents issued by or on behalf of the charity which solicit money or property for the charity's benefit;

- bills of exchange, promissory notes, endorsements, cheques and orders for money or goods purporting to be signed on the charity's behalf;

- bills, invoices, receipts and letters of credit.

Best practice is to state 'registered charity in England and Wales number XXXXXX'. The statement must be in English (except for Welsh charities which can use Welsh); however, if the charity normally uses another language the statement can appear in both English and that other language. The printing must be in legible characters.

Anyone who signs or issues or authorises the issue of a non-compliant item is liable to criminal penalties (fines) whether or not that person did so knowingly – it is a strict liability offence.

4.11.2 Charity disclosure obligations – Scotland

For charities subject to regulation in Scotland, regulations require a range of disclosures to be made (see the Charities References in Documents (Scotland) Regulations 2007 (SI 2007/203) as amended). In summary, these require inclusion on a wide range of documents of:

- the Scottish charity registration number;

- the name by which it is recorded on the Scottish Charity Register;

- an indication of its charitable status (if the word 'charity' or 'charitable' is not part of its name.

Relevant documents include letters, emails, adverts, notices and official publications, items soliciting money or property, invoices, receipts, accounts, campaign and educational documentation and documents relating to land transactions and contracts.

Note that an English charity also registered in Scotland must comply with both the English and the Scottish disclosure requirements.

Some practical difficulties have emerged in the application of the Scottish rules. There are likely to be some further changes in consequence but this involves amendment of the current regulations and will therefore take some while. In the meantime, the OSCR has issued helpful guidance on the application of these rules, which can be viewed at www.oscr.org.uk.

4.11.3   Company disclosure obligations

Company law applies disclosure obligations on all companies. For charitable companies, these obligations are in addition to their charity law disclosure obligations.

For the purposes of the tables below, 'company name' means the name of the company as on the company's certificate of incorporation, including 'Limited' or 'Ltd' (or their Welsh equivalents) and 'where registered' means 'England & Wales', 'Scotland' or 'Northern Ireland' according to the location of the registered office.

Whether on stationery, websites or premises, all disclosures must be in characters which can be read with the naked eye.

Stationery, websites, etc

	Company name	Where registered	Reg office address	Company number
Business letters	✓	✓	✓	✓
Order forms	✓	✓	✓	✓
Orders for goods, services or money	✓	✓	✓	✓
Cheques	✓			
Invoices and receipts	✓			
Notices and official publications	✓			
Bills of exchange, promissory notes, endorsements, bills of parcel and letters of credit	✓			
Written demands for payment of debts	✓			
Websites, order forms, emails and other electronic documents	✓	✓	✓	✓
Applications for licences to carry on a trade or activity	✓			

At premises, details must be positioned so they can be seen easily by visitors. The registered name must be displayed continuously unless the premises are shared by six or more companies. In that case, each company's name only needs to be displayed for at least 15 continuous seconds at least once in every 3 minutes – for example, where names are displayed electronically, in rotation.

There is no legal requirement for the company to display its certificate of incorporation at its registered office or any other premises.

Premises	
	Company name
The company's registered office (unless the company has always been dormant)	✓
Any 'inspection place', ie any location (other than the registered office) where the company keeps any company record available for public inspection (unless the company has always been dormant)	✓
Every location in which the company carries on business that is not the registered office or an 'inspection place' (unless primarily used for living accommodation or unless every director is protected from disclosure of their residential address to a credit reference agency)	✓

4.11.4 Statement of limited liability status

A company which has been granted permission to omit 'limited' from its name under the Companies Act 2006 (or the previous Companies Act 1985 rules) must state that it is a limited company on all business letters and order forms. The statement must be in English and in legible characters, the usual form is 'A company limited by guarantee'.

4.11.5 Other disclosures

Other legislation may impose additional requirements, these may be particularly relevant to stationery items. For example, if the organisation is registered for VAT, the VAT registration number must be printed on invoices and receipts.

4.11.6   Disclosures – practicalities and issues

Deciding which items are subject to a given set of legal rules is not always easy. Paper letter heading, invoices, receipts, demands for payment, orders for goods and services are certainly stationery items subject to relevant rules. However, emails, faxes, websites, compliments slips and business cards can be more problematic – at times it may depend on how they are used. For instance, such items could be used to place or receive an order or to record a contract between a third party and the organisation. A cautious approach is to include full statutory details on these 'problem' items.

Guidance should be given to staff, volunteers and local branches or remote offices which may be ordering or using stationery items (eg local event posters, fundraising literature, local group letter heading).

Independent groups or bodies should not be allowed to use a charity's name and charity registration number in a manner which might mislead the public into believing they were dealing with the charity itself rather than a separate organisation.

If there are any changes of name, care should be taken to ensure all old stationery is withdrawn and new stationery is used from the date of the change. Other items may also require attention, including electronic communications and websites. There are risks if this is not adequately dealt with, for instance potential personal liabilities for directors or any secretary of a company if a cheque is issued in the incorrect name.

Correct timing of such changes is important. A company's name only changes in law when the certificate of incorporation on change of name is issued (not on the date the change of name resolution is passed).

4.12   Execution of documents

Exactly how charities execute documents depends on:

* the legal nature of the charity (especially whether or not it is incorporated);
* the terms of the charity's constitution;
* the nature of the transaction to which the document relates (and any special legal rules that may apply to it); and
* the applicable jurisdictional law (whether it is a transaction under the law of England and Wales or Scotland or Northern Ireland).

The above factors affect the level of formality and detailed procedures required. It is important to observe the correct process and appropriate legal advice should be taken.

There is a useful statutory provision that enables the trustee board of an unincorporated charity to authorise any two or more trustees to execute documents in general, or a more limited range of documents, on behalf of the whole board (section 333 of the Charities Act 2011). Such execution gives effect to transactions to which all the trustees are legally a party. The authority must be given by the board as a whole. When a document is subsequently executed pursuant to that authority, a person who acquires an interest in, or charge on, property, or the benefit of a covenant or agreement, in good faith and for money or money's worth, is protected (see section 333(5) of the Charities Act 2011).

Charitable companies and trading subsidiaries need to observe the terms of their articles when executing documents (eg as to authorising use and countersignature of a company seal). In addition, the Companies Act 2006 provisions regarding execution of documents by companies should be noted. Those provisions state that a company can execute a document under the law of England and Wales by:

- fixing the company seal on the document; or

- executing without use of a seal, in accordance with the Companies Act 2006 procedure.

4.12.1   Company seal

A company may choose to have a company seal but is not obliged to do so. Initial adoption of a seal should be by formal resolution of the board. Subsequently, the company has a choice of executing documents with its seal or using the Companies Act 2006 alternative methods of execution for the particular item.

Use of the seal should be formally authorised, as should the countersignatories, the decisions should be recorded in the minutes of the relevant board meeting. Records should be kept of all items sealed – a register of sealings is useful (though not a statutory requirement). The seal itself should be kept in safe custody.

4.12.2   Execution of documents by companies without a seal under the law of England and Wales

The Companies Act 2006 permits execution of a document by a company, without a seal, if it is signed on behalf of the company by:

- two directors; or

- one director and the secretary; or

- one director in the presence of a witness, who attests the director's signature.

The decision to execute is a matter for the whole board, as is the authorisation of the chosen signatories. These decisions should be carefully recorded in the minutes of the relevant board meeting. The company may also choose to keep a non-statutory register of executions.

4.12.3   Execution of deeds – companies (under the law of England and Wales or Northern Ireland)

For certain legal transactions and arrangements it is appropriate or necessary to enter into a deed. A document is validly executed as a deed by a company, for the purposes of section 1(2)(b) of the Law of Property (Miscellaneous Provisions) Act 1989, and for the purposes of the law of Northern Ireland, if it is:

(a)   duly executed; and

(b)   delivered as a deed.

Delivery is presumed on execution unless the contrary is proved. A deed must contain appropriate wording, including the wording of its execution clause.

4.12.4   Execution of documents – other charities

Charities that are incorporated bodies but not companies must follow the procedures required by their own constitutions to execute documents.

Unincorporated charities execute documents (including deeds) in accordance with their own constitutions (usually by signature of all the trustees). There is a useful statutory power for the trustees of an unincorporated charity to authorise any two or more of the trustees to execute documents in the names of, and on behalf of, the trustees to give effect to a transaction to which all the trustees are a party (section 333 of the Charities Act 2011). The authority conferred may be general or limited as specified in the relevant trustees' decision (eg authority to execute on specific document, rather than documents in general). A further advantage of this procedure is that it avoids having to join in new trustees to a deed previously signed by all the former trustees.

4.12.5 Execution of documents under the law
of Scotland

The law of Scotland makes different provision for the execution of documents. The key provisions are in the Requirements of Writing (Scotland) Act 1995 and, in the context of companies, section 48 of the Companies Act 2006. Specific Scottish legal advice should be taken where appropriate.

4.12.6 Records of sealings and executions

Board decisions to enter into contracts, authorise the use of the charity's seal or otherwise authorise execution of documents (including deeds) should be properly recorded in the minutes of the relevant board meeting. Where specific signatories are authorised, the minutes should include details of that decision and the names of the relevant individuals. It is good practice to record each use of the seal, or execution of a document without a seal, in an optional register of sealings and Executions and to ensure a full copy of the sealed or executed document is also retained.

4.12.7 Authentication of documents and information –
Companies Act 2006 rules

The Companies Act 2006 uses the term 'authenticated' widely in relation to documents and information sent to a person by a company or supplied by a person to a company. It does so for both hard copy and electronic formats. The legal rules specify:

• A hard copy item is authenticated if it is signed by the person sending or supplying it.

• An item in electronic form is authenticated if:

 – the identity of the sender is confirmed in a manner prescribed by the company; or

 – where no such manner has been specified, if the communication contains or is accompanied by a statement of the identity of the sender and the company has no reason to doubt the truth of that statement.

(See section 1146 of the Companies Act 2006.)

4.13   Electronic signatures and electronic communications

The use of electronic communications is widespread and can assist the efficient operation and management of a charity. Fundamental underlying legal rules and principles generally apply, in areas such as the limits of the charity's charitable purposes and powers, legal authority and the law of contract. It is also important to be aware that:

- disclosure obligations under charity law and company law extend to electronic communications (for instance emails sent by or on behalf of a charity or a company) and websites; and

- in some situations, additional regulations relating to electronic communications and e-commerce may apply.

There is general legal provision relating to electronic communications and electronic signatures in the Electronic Communications Act 2000.

For companies, there are significant rules in the Companies Act 2006 addressing electronic communications:

- *to* a company *by an individual member* (Schedule 4);

- *by* a company (either to its own members or from a corporate member to the company of which it is a member) (Schedule 5).

The Schedules cited above apply regardless of anything in the company's articles. Their requirements are detailed and complex. Care should be taken to interpret and apply them correctly in all formal company/member communications (such as communications relating to general meetings of the members, or providing access to the annual accounts and reports of the company).

Note also the Companies Act 2006 rules regarding 'authentication' of documents and information (see para 4.12.7).

5 Public Accountability and Reporting

5.1 Introduction

Public accountability is an important *quid pro quo* for the benefits of incorporated legal form and the protection of limited liability. Therefore, companies are listed on a public index held by the Registrar of Companies, and company law has always imposed a range of public accountability and public reporting requirements on companies.

The public accountability of charities reflects that they exist for the greater good of society as a whole. A charity exists to provide appropriate public benefit, through activities undertaken in pursuit of the charitable purposes set out in its constitution. It has funds and assets given to it (or otherwise acquired by it) that are held in order to pursue those purposes and provide that benefit. The law therefore imposes a wide range of controls and safeguards to ensure that is done properly. A major part of those controls and safeguards features accountability, in one or more forms.

Accountability is largely a public matter, requiring companies and charities to make information available in a very public form and to answer to one or more regulatory bodies, themselves publicly funded, to ensure that the public's interests are protected and risks to creditors and other third parties are controlled. In the case of charities, an overriding aim of the legal requirements is to ensure charitable assets are safeguarded and properly applied. The public availability of annual accounts and reports enables the public at large to see this is the case.

5.1.1 Accountability of charities – the stakeholders

There are a number of potential stakeholders in relation to charity accountability, they include:

- The relevant charity regulators. The Charity Commission, for registered charities in England and Wales, the OSCR for all charities on the Scottish Charity Register (including 'foreign' charities on that register, such as a charity registered in England and Wales that also operates in Scotland) and the

Charity Commission for Northern Ireland for charities in Northern Ireland.

- The courts (the High Court in England and Wales, the Court of Session in Scotland, the High Court in Northern Ireland). Ultimately they act on the Crown's behalf as public guardians of charitable assets.

- The general public, because all charities exist to provide public benefit.

- The charity's membership (in a membership charity).

- The current and future beneficiaries. Trustees must balance the interests of both in their management of the charity and its resources, ensuring the organisation's future viability.

The concept of accountability to beneficiaries is easier to comprehend where the direct beneficiaries of the particular activities are human, whether people in general or a defined portion of the population. It is a little more difficult to grasp where the charity exists to benefit people indirectly, for example through activities that protect and enhance the environment or provide for the care and welfare of animals or plants.

Accountability may also be due to others, for instance one or more additional regulators that have jurisdiction over the particular charity, because of its particular legal form or its particular activities. Examples might include Companies House, the Care Quality Commission (for England and Wales) or Care Inspectorate (for Scotland), the Homes and Communities Agency and the Regulator of Social Housing (also known as the Tenant Services Authority).

5.1.2   Accountability of charities – trustees' responsibilities

Charity trustees are given particular responsibilities in the context of accountability. For all charities, whatever their legal form, the trustees have obligations relating to public accountability. These particularly arise from charity law, which demands the preparation and public filing of detailed information about charities, their trustees, their activities, circumstances, finances, funds and assets and their strategies and plans – both current and future.

Public accountability through public filing is imposed in two ways:

- Through 'event'-related public filing obligations. Certain events must be notified to the Charity Commission and some changes also require the Commission's advance consent (eg a change to the charitable purposes). Charitable companies also have obligations to publicly notify specified events to Companies House, because of obligations arising under company law.

- Through the annual filing of accounts and the trustees' report and the charity annual return. Changes amongst the trustees, through appointments or resignations, need to be notified on the annual update which is filed as part of the charity annual return. Reporting obligations are wider than was once the case, especially in relation to reporting of the public benefit that charities deliver.

Some charities have further public accountability, through 'event' or annual filing obligations arising from other statutory provisions. Examples of this are the obligations for charitable companies to:

- file their SORP and Companies Act 2006 compliant annual accounts and reports and their company annual return at Companies House;

- file 'event'-related forms and documents (eg special resolutions of their members, forms notifying the passing of certain types of members' resolutions (such as a change of objects), alterations to the names or rights of membership classes, changes amongst the directors or changes to serving directors' details).

- keep statutory registers that are open for public inspection (eg the register of directors and secretaries and the register of members).

5.2   Annual compliance

Companies, CICs and charities (including SCIOs and CIOs) are all subject to various compulsory annual compliance obligations, requiring annual accounts and reports and certain returns to be filed with appropriate regulators. The rules about the form and contents of some of these items are detailed and in many cases complex. A brief overview is given below but the reader should be aware that there is much more detail than space allows this book to address.

The Companies Act 2006 and its associated regulations apply throughout the UK, so all companies (including CICs) are subject to the company law annual accountability requirements, regardless of the jurisdiction in which they are registered.

For charities, the annual accountability requirements differ between the three jurisdictions (England and Wales, Scotland, Northern Ireland). Whilst some of the differences in the accounting and reporting requirements that affect charitable companies, compared to other legal forms of charities, have been removed by recent reforms, important differences remain (eg in exemption thresholds and in the underlying format of the annual accounts – companies must produce accounts on an accruals basis, not a receipts and payments basis). Some aspects of the time limits and penalty regimes for non-compliance also differ.

It is very important that specialist professional advice is taken, from advisers experienced in relevant areas, to ensure an organisation meets all the annual compliance obligations relevant to its size and legal form.

5.2.1   General annual compliance – companies (company law requirements)

Every company must file a company annual return form every year (section 854 of the Companies Act 2006). This is made up to the date of incorporation (or the date of the last return if different) and must be filed within 28 days of that date (the made up to date is known as the 'return date'). A fee is payable, which is at a reduced level if the return is filed online.

The information required from companies limited by guarantee on the company annual return is quite straightforward. They do not have to provide lists of their members or details about changes in their membership during the year. The precise contents and style of the form are subject to periodic change.

Every company must also file its annual accounts and reports within 9 months of the financial year end. There is no filing fee (note the difference compared to the position for reporting by CICs (see para 5.2.2)).

The penalty levels for non-compliance with the accounts filing deadline have been considerably increased by the Companies Act 2006. These are civil penalties, automatically levied by Companies House when the late delivery of the accounts occurs (no court action is necessary).

The table below provides a summary of the financial penalties, for accounts of private companies filed late on or after 1 February 2009 (the Companies (Late Filing Penalties) and Limited Liability Partnerships (Filing Periods and Late Filing Penalties) Regulations 2008 (SI 2008/497)). In cases where there was also a failure to meet the deadline in a previous financial year that began on or after 6 April 2008, the second year penalty is doubled.

How late	*Penalty*
Not more than 1 month	£150
Over 1 month, not more than 3 months	£375
Over 3 months, not more than 6 months	£750
More than 6 months	£1,500

5.2.2 Additional annual compliance – community interest companies

A CIC must also provide a 'community interest report' annually (section 34 of the Companies (Audit, Investigations and Community Enterprise) Act 2004). It is made publicly available (through Companies House). The report must contain specified information, such as a description of the activities that have been undertaken for the benefit of the community, details of directors' remuneration and other benefits and information about how the CIC's stakeholders have been consulted. A statutory fee is payable to the CIC Regulator when the report is filed.

The report is included with the annual accounts and other required reports that are prepared and submitted to the Registrar of Companies. The Registrar then provides a copy to the CIC Regulator who monitors the report to ensure the CIC continues to meet the community interest test. The information provided by the CIC will, of course, be considered in the light of its objects, set out in its articles, the applicable 'asset lock' and the other regulatory controls on the application of a CIC's funds and other assets.

5.2.3 Additional annual compliance – charities

In addition to preparing and filing accounts, charities must file a charity annual return under relevant charities legislation, unless they fall below the relevant thresholds (which are subject to alteration). This is filed with the appropriate charity regulator, the Charity Commission and/or the OSCR. The forms for each jurisdiction are different and are also subject to frequent changes. In the case of a 'cross-border' charity, registered on both charity registers, a return must be made in each jurisdiction in accordance with that jurisdiction's legal requirements.

Larger charities in England and Wales (income over £1 million per annum) must also submit further information on a summary information return (SIR). The SIR is part of their charity annual return and is made publicly available on the Charity Commission website (www.charitycommission.gov.uk).

Note that these charity annual compliance requirements apply regardless of the particular charity's legal form.

There will be similar annual requirements for charities in Northern Ireland as the relevant Northern Ireland charity law comes into force (probably during 2012/13).

5.2.4 Checklist of annual filing requirements (charitable companies)

The following abbreviations are used in this checklist:

CA 2006	Companies Act 2006
ChA 2011	Charities Act 2011
SORP	*Accounting and Reporting by Charities: Statement of Recommended Practice, 2005*

1. Companies House – annual return

Annual return form AR01 made up to 'return date'.

File every year within 28 days from return date with statutory fee. Note a lower fee applies if the return is filed online (eg via Companies House 'web filing' option).

'Return date' is the anniversary of the date of incorporation or the anniversary of the last annual return (if earlier).

2. Companies House – annual accounts and reports

Annual accounts and reports made up to 'accounting reference date'.

For an accounting reference period from day after last year's accounting reference date to accounting reference date in this year (ie a financial year). First accounting reference period, however, commences on date of incorporation.

'Accounting reference date' is automatically last day of month in which company was incorporated unless altered by filing form AA01.

Form, layout and contents vary according to size of company and whether it is audit exempt or subject to independent examination of its annual accounts or to compulsory audit. The directors' report should meet CA 2006 directors' report requirements for a company limited by guarantee and ChA 2011 (with associated accounts and reports regulations), and SORP requirements for the trustees' report (or Scottish equivalents for charities subject to the law of Scotland).

File within 9 months of accounting reference date (special rules for first accounts – if for period exceeding 12 months file by *later* of 21 months after incorporation date *or* 3 months after accounting reference date).

Company name and registered company number must be shown, *original* signatures required on balance sheet and directors' report.

If the accounts have been audited or independently examined, the auditor's report/examiner's report must be signed.

NB all signatures must be in black ink (hard copy items).

Civil penalties against company if filed late, possible criminal penalties against directors.

3. Charity Commission – charity annual return and trustee detail update/accounts (England and Wales)

File annually. Charity annual return is a different form to company annual return.

Annual return and trustee details update are sent to charitable company by the Charity Commission for checking, completion and return.

All charitable companies with annual income over £10,000 must file it. Lower income charities are encouraged to provide an 'annual update' to the Commission to ensure it has up-to-date records of the charity.

A charity annual return must be accompanied by the annual accounts and trustees' report.

Note the amount of detail required on an annual return form varies according to the charity's annual income:

£10,001–£25,000	Charity information including contact, trustee details, income and expenditure information
£25,001–£500,000	Charity information as above, Reporting serious incidents, plus a copy of the annual accounts and trustees' report, with auditors' report/independent examiner's report
£500,001–£1 million	As immediately above, plus additional financial information
Over £1 million	As immediately above, plus SIR No fee payable

Online filing is available via the Charity Commission website (www.charitycommission.gov.uk). NB the paper alternative is to be withdrawn.

Default – potential criminal penalties against officers. The Charity Commission records late filing on the charity's public record.

4. Charitable companies – Scotland: charity annual return

Charities on the Scottish Charity Register must file a charity annual return in accordance with the requirements of the Charities and Trustee Investment (Scotland) Act 2005 and associated regulations. The relevant form is supplied to the charity by the OSCR, it must be completed in black ink and filed with the OSCR, accompanied by the charity's annual accounts. The OSCR uses the annual return as a key method of monitoring charities, analysis of the information provided can therefore trigger queries from the OSCR if there are apparent areas of concern.

If the charity has annual income greater than £25,000, it must also provide a supplementary monitoring return providing additional information to the OSCR (mainly financial information).

5.3 Accounting records

All charities need accurate, up-to-date accounting records for a range of practical as well as legal reasons. These include managing cash flow, ensuring solvency, budgeting, financial controls and monitoring, asset recording and security and the overall effective management of the charity and its resources. Such information helps the trustees fulfil their legal responsibilities for the charity and be accountable for their stewardship of it. The internal accounting records also facilitate the preparation of accurate public annual accounts and reports.

The accounting records are open to all trustees and to the charity's auditor or independent examiner but are not public documents (unlike the annual accounts, which are publicly accessible). The accounting records are not required by law to be open to the wider membership of the charity, unless the particular charity's constitution provides for members' access (which is unusual).

The legal requirements for the accounting records of companies are summarised below. Similar standards apply to the records of other legal forms of charities. The records must:

- record and explain all transactions, including receipts and expenditures, and the reasons for them;

- disclose the present financial position with reasonable accuracy; and

- enable the trustees to ensure the annual accounts meet the statutory requirements for those accounts.

Accounting records should be retained for at least 6 years. Some records may need to be kept for longer periods due to specific statutory or regulatory requirements relevant to the particular charity.

5.3.1   Accounting records – Scotland

Charity law in Scotland requires charities on the Scottish Charity Register to keep accounting records that disclose:

- the day-to-day funds received and spent;

- assets and liabilities of the charity; and

- the charity's current financial position.

These must enable the charity to prepare annual accounts that comply with Scottish charity public reporting requirements.

5.4   Annual accounting and reporting – charities

The standards to which charities must provide public annual accounts and reports are significantly higher than those applicable to comparable sized commercial organisations. The precise technical detail of the contents, both from a legal and an accounting perspective, varies according to the charity's legal form and its financial size (especially its annual income from all sources). There are also differences in requirements between the three UK jurisdictions.

Subject to those caveats, the principles of public reporting are largely dealt with by the charities SORP. The charities SORP provides a definitive code of best practice for 'true and fair view' annual financial reporting and is broadly compulsory. For some charities in particular fields, such as higher and further education colleges, social housing organisations and Church of England Parochial Church Councils, there are 'sub-sector' specific SORPs.

The general SORP regime for charity accounts and reports provides for a statement of financial activities (SOFA) during the year; a balance sheet as at the financial year end; a trustees' report and various notes to the statutory accounts.

The SOFA records all incoming and outgoing resources during the year in a columnar format. The various different types of funds must be shown separately (for further details, see para 5.4.2). Previous year comparator figures are also required. The balance sheet indicates the end of year financial position. The trustees' report provides some commentary on the figures, to provide clarity of understanding, and enables the trustees to report more widely on their stewardship of the charity.

Annual accounts are required by law to give a 'true and fair view' and must therefore be prepared on the 'going concern' assumption and on an accruals basis (the latter is subject to exceptions for smaller non-corporate charities). The information they provide must be relevant, reliable, comparable and understandable. In the preparation of the accounts, consideration must be given to relevant accounting standards issued or adopted by the Accounting Standards Board (in addition to the charities SORP standards, of course).

Additional requirements apply to charities with subsidiary or associated companies and charities that have particular trust funds under their control (sometimes described as 'special trusts').

Note that in a charitable company the Companies Act 2006 requirements for a directors' report can be included within the trustees' report. It is not necessary to prepare two separate reports.

There are 'lighter touch' obligations for smaller charities in the overall accounting and reporting requirements. The Charity Commission estimates that at least 85% of charities can benefit from those.

5.4.1   Annual accounting and reporting – Scotland and Northern Ireland

Charities on the Scottish Charity Register are generally subject to public accounting and reporting requirements arising from the Charities and Trustee Investment (Scotland) Act 2005 and the Charities Accounts (Scotland) Regulations 2006 (SI 2006/218) (as amended). Special provisions for SCIOs enable them to opt to prepare receipts and payments accounts (rather than accruals-based accounts) if their annual income is below £500,000.

An accounting and reporting regime for charities in Northern Ireland is being introduced under the Charities Act (Northern Ireland) 2008. Detailed regulations have yet to be made and the implementation date is therefore not yet known.

In both jurisdictions, charities in the legal form of a company limited by guarantee are required to submit their annual accounts and reports to Companies House, as well as their charity regulator(s).

5.4.2   Fund accounting

Charities must account correctly for the different types of funds they hold and for particular trust funds they hold. Those trust funds must be separately and properly administered in accordance with the terms of the particular trust. So the charity's accounting records must explain all transactions on each such fund and the annual accounts must report each fund, indicate the nature of the trust, and record activities during the year as well as opening and closing balances and any transfers between funds.

In order to manage and apply the charity's funds correctly, as well as record and report them correctly, trustees need to understand the differences between various fund types and to identify and observe relevant restrictions imposed by trusts over particular funds.

Unrestricted funds are funds that are not subject to legal restrictions as to their use. They are freely available to be applied by the trustees for any lawful activity within the charity's purposes and powers.

There may be unspent funds with the unrestricted funds that the trustees have earmarked for particular purposes. These are sometimes called designated funds. They do not have to be separately accounted for, as they are not legally bound to spent in that way, the trustees are free to change their plans and deploy the funds in alternative ways (eg if a particular project envisaged does not in fact proceed). Where significant amounts are being held in reserves towards future planned expenditure, appropriate explanations should be set out in the trustees' report about why the funds are being held and when they are expected to be applied to the relevant project or activity.

Restricted funds are subject to restrictions on their use (ie subject to particular trusts) and must be used within the terms of the relevant restriction. Usually the restriction comes from the donor, in the terms of the gift (eg a bequest under a will) or because the charity appealed for gifts for a specified purpose. It is essential that restricted funds are 'ring-fenced' and used for the correct purposes. They cannot be used to subsidise other funds or applied to the charity's general running costs. Breaches of the restrictions will amount to breaches of trust, with significant consequences which can include personal liability for the trustees.

If it is not possible to apply restricted funds to the particular restricted purpose, the original donor's consent may be sought to apply them for alternative specific purposes within the charity's general charitable purposes, or simply to allow them to be used towards those general purposes. If that is impractical or impossible, perhaps because the donor is untraceable or dead, there are various legal processes by which the restrictions may be able to be altered or relaxed. The trustees must ensure they have appropriate legal authority before applying the funds in an alternative way.

Endowments are capital funds, where the capital is invested in order to generate expendable income. Some endowments funds are permanent endowment, where the capital value must be retained (even if the particular assets that represent it, such as the mix of investments, alter). The legal restrictions that make the funds permanent endowment normally arise at the point of original gift, for example when a bequest to the charity takes effect. If matters are not clear it may be necessary to take legal advice and perhaps consult the Charity Commission for guidance. Permanent endowment is more common in older unincorporated charitable trusts. If a charitable company created as a successor, to take over the funds, assets and activities of an older unincorporated charity, acquires endowed funds from that predecessor, the charitable company will become the corporate trustee of the funds and is obliged to retain the capital value of the endowment.

5.4.3   SORP compliance

The charities SORP is particularly aimed at those who prepare, audit or examine annual accounts of charities and is therefore largely written in technical accounting language. Some parts of it are therefore not readily understood by those with little knowledge or experience of accounting principles, practices and standards for financial reporting. Nonetheless, it is important to recognise that the trustees remain responsible for ensuring the charity complies with annual reporting obligations. Further, since the trustees are collectively responsible for the safeguarding and correct application of the charity's resources, they must ensure the annual accounts and trustees' report adequately reflect all those resources and the use made of them in pursuit of the charity's charitable purposes during the year reported on.

Save for charities for which sub-sector SORPs apply and smaller charities which can take advantage of some 'lighter touch' relaxations, all charities are expected by both the Charity Commission and the OSCR to comply fully with the SORP standards in their accounting and reporting. Where there is a departure from SORP, the regulators expect that departure to be identified and an adequate explanation given.

5.4.4 Summary information return/supplementary monitoring return

The largest charities in England and Wales (annual income above £1 million in the *previous* financial year) are also obliged to provide an SIR to the Charity Commission each year. This is provided to accompany the charity annual return. Both may be filed together online. The SIR provides a range of data items, partially repeating information from the annual accounts. The data must relate to the group, not simply the individual charity (so it includes gross figures for the charity plus its subsidiaries, whether those are charitable subsidiaries or trading companies). The SIR is a public document and can be accessed on the Charity Commission website (www.charitycommission.gov.uk), along with the charity's annual accounts and trustees' report.

Charities on the Scottish Charity Register with income above £25,000 must provide a supplementary monitoring return to the OSCR. This provides additional information to supplement their charity annual return (mainly financial data).

5.4.5 Trustees' annual report

With some exceptions for the smallest charities, there must be an annual trustees' report (section 162 of the Charities Act 2011). The contents of this report are specified by the charities SORP, with more substantial requirements for larger charities (income over £500,000 and therefore subject to statutory audit obligations). Whilst the major areas the report *must* cover are set out in the SORP it should be noted that:

- the trustees of any charity may add further material if they wish;

- small charities can opt to include the higher level of detail required of larger charities;

- the order in which the material is set out is not obligatory (therefore the 'boring legal detail' of administrative information and legal disclosures, such as lists of professional advisers, need not be the opening statements).

The trustees' report requirements recognise that numbers are not, of themselves, enough to show the overall picture of a charity's activities and its end of year position. Even more importantly, the figures cannot tell the story of the public benefit that has been provided and the good that the charity is doing. Imaginative trustees' reports certainly can.

The trustees are responsible for the contents of the report and their accuracy. The board as a whole must formally approve the report and authorise its signature by one trustee on behalf of the board.

Whilst the exact contents required in the trustees' report vary according the size of the charity, the following checklist provides the broad framework of contents. Note again the earlier comments about how the material is presented and the trustees' freedom to elaborate on basic requirements.

5.4.6   Checklist of contents – trustees' annual report

1. Public benefit

A trustees' annual report must include:

(a)   a report of those activities undertaken by a charity to further its charitable purposes for the public benefit; and

(b)   a statement by the charity trustees as to whether they have complied with the duty in section 17(5) of the Charities Act 2011 to 'have regard' to public benefit guidance published by the Commission.

Note that a number of different Charity Commission guidance notes have been issued with regard to public benefit, all of which can be obtained from the Charity Commission's website (www.charitycommision.gov.uk). The trustees of all charities should take note of the main guidance: *Charities and public benefit*. The trustees of charities to which any of the additional guidance notes are relevant should also consider the following: *Public Benefit and Fee Charging*, *The Advancement of Education for the Public Benefit*, *The*

Advancement of Religion for the Public Benefit and *The Prevention or Relief of Poverty for the Public Benefit.*

2. Reference and administrative material about the charity, its trustees and advisers

This section must give the charity's full legal name (as on the relevant charity register) plus any other name by which it is known (eg an operational name) and the charity registration number. If the charity is registered in both England and Wales and Scotland, the two numbers will be different (the Scottish charity number will be prefixed 'SC'). If the charity is in the legal form of a company, its company number must also be stated.

The address of the principal office must be given and, for a charitable company, the address of its registered office.

The names of all trustees must be stated, which should include all who served for any part of the year being reported on. If trustees have joined the board after that year but before the approval of the report, their names should also be given.

The name of the chief executive officer and the names of any staff to whom the trustees have delegated day-to-day management must be given (ie senior management staff).

Names and addresses of all relevant professional advisers must be stated (eg solicitors, bankers, auditors or reporting accountants/ independent examiners, investment advisers).

3. Structure, governance and management

This section must set out the legal form of the charity (unincorporated charitable trust, unincorporated members' association, charitable company limited by guarantee, etc); specify the nature of the governing document (eg constitution, trust deed or articles of association); and set out the methods for appointing trustees.

There should be details of how new trustees are inducted, plus information about the general training and development of trustees.

The organisational structure must be described (eg committees and their roles, in the context of the governance role of the trustee board) and the decision-making processes explained.

If the charity is part of a wider network, information should be given about that.

Details of relationships with related parties must be given. Note that the charities SORP defines 'related parties'.

There must be a statement about risk management, including the review processes by which risks are identified and the systems and procedures adopted by the board to manage those risks.

4. Objectives and activities

This section should make clear the aims and objectives set by the charity; the strategies and activities undertaken to achieve them; and put matters in the context of the longer-term strategies and objectives that have been set.

The information must include a summary of the charitable purposes (as set out in the governing document); an explanation of the charity's aims, including what changes or differences it seeks to make by its activities; an explanation of the main objectives for the year being reported on and the strategies for achieving the stated objectives, as well as details of significant activities that contribute to obtaining the objectives.

If the charity makes grants as a major activity, the grant-making policy must be stated.

If there are material social investment programmes and/or material use of volunteers, information must be provided about those areas.

5. Achievements and performance

This section must give information about the achievements of the charity (and any subsidiaries) during the year being reported on. In particular it should review the charitable activities, explaining performance against objectives, give details of material fundraising activities, again including performance achieved against objectives set and commenting on material expenditure as well as projected future income.

Details of material investments and their performance against the investment objectives should be given.

Any factors outside the charity's control that are relevant to the achievement of its objectives should be commented upon. These might include relationships with employees, service users, other beneficiaries and funders and the charity's position in the wider community.

6. Financial review

A review of the charity's financial position is required (and that of any subsidiaries). The principal financial management policies adopted during the year should be stated.

The policy on financial reserves, the level of reserves held and why they are held must be indicated. If material sums have been designated for particular purposes, the amounts and reasons must be given, together with intended timing of future expenditure. If there is a deficit or surplus on the target reserves sums, this must be indicted, together with the steps being taken to address the difference.

Principal funding sources must be given.

There must be information about how expenditure during the year has supported the charity's key objectives.

If there are material investments, the investment policy and its objectives, including any social, environmental or ethical considerations, should be indicated.

7. Plans for future periods

The charity's plans for future periods need to be explained, including key aims and objectives and details of activities planned to support these.

8. Funds held as custodian trustee

If the charity holds any funds in the capacity of 'custodian trustee', details must be given.

5.4.7 Public benefit reporting

There are compulsory reporting requirements regarding public benefit. The trustees' annual report must deal with two areas in this respect:

- set out a statement that the trustees have complied with their responsibility under section 17(5) of the Charities Act 2011 to have due regard to Charity Commission guidance on public benefit; and

- report on the charity's activities and achievements in relation to its charitable purposes for the public benefit.

Although some charities have opted to include a separate paragraph on public benefit in their trustees' report, it is far better to ensure the entire report speaks clearly of the benefit provided, as that is the *raison d'etre* of every charity. The good the organisation does, why that matters and how it helps both specific beneficiaries and wider society, should shine through the entire report – and be presented in engaging and lively terms, accessible to the general non-specialist reader (who is a potential new supporter of the charity).

Larger charities must review significant activities to further their charitable purposes or to raise funds to generate resources to do so, with details of annual aims, objectives and strategies, plus comments on achievements. Smaller charities can give a brief summary of activities and achievements.

Compliance with these obligations is improving, however far too many charities still make only a token effort, adding a few rather bland sentences to their trustee's report. Charity Commission surveys also show that a substantial number of trustee boards forget to make the required statement about having 'had regard' to the Commission's public benefit guidance.

5.4.8   External scrutiny of annual accounts

The external scrutiny of annual accounts has been largely harmonised for all legal forms of charities in England and Wales by recent reforms.

For a company, auditors must be appointed for each financial year unless the company is within a relevant audit exemption threshold *and* its directors reasonably resolve that such appointment is not necessary on the ground that audited accounts are unlikely to be required (section 485 of the Companies Act 2006). Audit exemption thresholds are affected by a number of factors, including turnover (or gross income level in a charity), balance sheet total and 'small company' status or membership of a group.

A charitable company that falls within applicable audit exemption thresholds (gross income under £500,000 or £250,000 if gross assets are more than £3.26 million), can have an independent examination on its accounts, instead of an audit. If its income is very small (under £25,000), no external scrutiny is obligatory under statutory provisions. In both cases, this is provided its own constitution does not impose an audit requirement.

Different thresholds and exemption provisions apply under charity law in Scotland. Detailed regulations have yet to be made for Northern Ireland.

Whilst external scrutiny of annual accounts is important, trustees should never over-rely on it. They should recognise that there is no substitute for sound financial management and adequate internal controls on a day-to-day basis. Nor is there any substitute for an organisation-wide culture of openness and transparency. In addition, the relevant independent scrutiny report should also be preceded in the annual accounts and reports by a good quality trustees' report.

The external scrutiny requirements and exemption thresholds are as follows (charities in England and Wales). Note the statutory provisions regarding audit exemption and alternative independent examination are permissive, not overriding. If the charity's constitution requires an audit that requirement must be followed, as outlined in the following table:

Statutory audit or other report on the accounts	Size criteria – charitable companies	Size criteria – other charities
None	Gross income ceiling £25,000	Gross income ceiling £25,000*
Report by an independent examiner**	Gross income ceiling £500,000	Gross income ceiling £500,000
Full statutory audit report: Charities Act 2011 (as amended)	Gross income over £500,000 (£250,000 if book value of gross assets over £3.26m) or else no 'company audit exemption' claim	Gross income of charity or group over £500,000 (£250,000 if book value of gross assets over £3.26m)
Full statutory audit report: Companies Act 2006	Thresholds: turnover £6.5m; gross assets £3.26m; 50 staff (or 'audit exemption' unclaimed)	Not applicable

* For Church of England Parochial Church Councils, independent scrutiny is required under church accounting regulations.

** The independent examiner must be suitably qualified, in accordance with relevant regulations, if the charity's gross income exceeded £250,000.

5.4.9 Accounting and reporting – the charity regulators

The charity regulators monitor compliance with accounting and reporting requirements and with applicable time limits for submission of these items. They expect charities to meet their obligations and will take action when major non-compliance occurs. For example, the Charity Commission clearly flags up on a charity's public record when items have been submitted late. This is not good for the particular charity's standing and reputation with its beneficiaries, donors, other funders and supporters or the general public.

The regulators also monitor key matters about charities by reviewing the contents of the annual accounts and reports, in particular in areas such as:

- public benefit;
- charitable purposes and the proper pursuit of these;
- conflicts of interest;
- correct application of funds and assets;
- improper trading activities by the charity itself or improper dealings with a trading subsidiary;
- improper payments to or benefits for trustees and improper transactions with trustees and connected persons.

5.4.10 Public accessibility of annual accounts and reports

Annual accounts and reports are generally public documents and readily accessible in the public domain (if the charity is large enough to be within compulsory filing thresholds). The Charity Commission makes filed accounts and reports available on its website with free access, whilst low cost access via Companies House website is possible in relation to charitable companies and trading subsidiaries of charities. The OSCR does not yet make filed accounts and reports available on its website but it may do so in the future.

Members of a charitable company are entitled to receive full copies of the accounts and reports (section 423 of the Companies Act 2006). These must be provided not later than:

- the end of the period allowed for filing at Companies House; or
- if earlier, the date on which the accounts and reports are actually filed (section 424 of the Companies Act 2006).

Members of the public can also make a direct request for copies of any charity's annual accounts and reports.

Increasingly, many charities that have a website choose to make their latest accounts and trustees' report available to the public on that site, usually as a downloadable PDF. This is a commendably positive and transparent approach to their public accountability.

6 Finance and Funding

6.1 Finance and funding – general matters

There are certain key legal, taxation and practical issues relevant to the finances and funding of almost all charities and not-for-profit organisations. In addition, there will be other issues that arise because of:

- the legal form of the individual organisation; and

- any particular legal status it has (eg charity, CIC, etc).

Examples of important areas that are common to all organisations include constitutional powers and restrictions, as well as correct decision-making (through the right decision-making body). Other examples include appropriate monitoring of performance against budgets, cash flow forecasting, monitoring and maintaining solvency and the implementation of suitable internal financial controls and safeguards, plus anti-fraud/anti-money laundering safeguards and other preventative and deterrent measures against crime-related risks.

6.1.1 Accounting records

All organisations need to keep internal accounting records for their effective management and practical operation. A company must keep such records in accordance with Companies Act 2006 requirements. Charities must ensure their records meet the requirements of relevant charity law. Where statutory obligations to prepare public annual accounts apply, the internal records must facilitate compliance with that public accountability obligation. For further comments, see Chapter 5.

6.1.2 Funding

Increasingly, civil society organisations need a mix of funding sources in order to meet their funding needs. For charities, voluntary income remains a key part of their funding, through one-off donations, regular committed giving by individuals and organisations and legacies. In many cases if an individual donor is a UK taxpayer, the donations can be made in a tax-efficient manner, so the charity reclaims the basic rate of tax on the sum donated. For lifetime donations by higher rate taxpayers under the Gift Aid scheme, there is currently also some tax relief for individual donors, against their higher rate personal tax. Corporate donors (ie companies) making Gift Aid donations give the sum gross to the recipient charity, receiving an allowance against their corporation tax computation.

Other possible sources of funding include those listed below. However, it should be noted that not all of these would necessarily be available to a particular organisation due to its legal form or legal status (charity, CIC, etc) or because of other restrictions, including constitutional and statutory restrictions.

Possible sources of funding:

- grant funding from charities, philanthropic bodies or public sources;

- earned income from direct charitable activities (the 'contract culture' and pressures on the public finances have led to a considerable increase in the number of charities contracting to provide charitable services, often these were previously at least partially grant funded by public bodies, local authorities and the like);

- income from fundraising trading (often via a wholly owned trading subsidiary);

- social enterprise activities that generate a surplus;

- loans (commercial loans or low interest/interest free loans from supporters of the charity);

- fundraising initiatives (of many types, which bring a variety of legal, tax and VAT, risk, reporting and other issues to address);

- membership income (eg fees, annual subscriptions);

- third party investment/venture capital and similar commercial or semi-commercial funding;*

- share capital.*

   * This may be found in some social enterprises and some CICs but is not normally an appropriate, or even possible, source of funding in a charity.

6.1.3 Fundraising

Fundraising is not capable of being a charitable purpose in law and fundraising is not, in itself, a charitable activity. This is true even when the funds raised are applied entirely for charitable activities.

Active fundraising, from particular organisations and bodies or from the general public, is commonly undertaken by many charities and not-for-profit organisations. There are many different ways in which this is done – and many different legal and tax implications of those varied methods.

In many cases, a wide range of regulatory restrictions and obligations will apply to the methods and techniques being used, especially in the case of fundraising for charities.

In Scotland, fundraising regulations also extend to fundraising for any 'benevolent body' (ie a body set up for benevolent or philanthropic purposes (the Charities and Benevolent Fundraising (Scotland) Regulations 2009 (SI 2009/121)).

6.1.4   Fundraising consultants

When a charity considers using third parties to assist in fundraising, it should be clear about the nature of the proposed relationship. Consider whether the charity is seeking to engage:

- an external consultant who will not engage in the act of fundraising him- or herself; or

- a professional fundraiser who will directly undertake fundraising activities on the charity's behalf, ie engage in the act of fundraising.

A true 'fundraising consultant' is a person paid by a charity to advise it on fundraising but who does not him- or herself make a solicitation on behalf of the charity for money or property. Instead, the individual may draft publicity and advertising material, research potential donors and advise on how to target and approach them ('making the ask'), help write funding applications and grant bids, advise on funding or fundraising strategies, etc.

Provided the consultant has no direct contact with the donors, his or her activities are likely to be outside the regulatory regime for 'professional fundraisers' in Part II of the Charities Act 1992. Those paid fundraisers who do actually solicit money or other property on the charity's behalf, expressly or impliedly, will be subject to the controls laid down in the legislation cited above (see para 6.2).

6.1.5   In-house fundraising

Fundraising initiatives dealt with in-house, by employees of charities and volunteers (and by a charity's wholly owned subsidiary), will not *per se* be subject to the 'professional fundraiser' or 'commercial participant' fundraising regulatory requirements. However, care is needed in analysing exactly how the fundraising is to be carried out and how the proceeds generated will be dealt with, as the detailed arrangements may involve compliance with those regulations (eg if a third party is to receive the funds on the charity's behalf).

6.2 Fundraising regulation – general

Modern regulatory regimes are being introduced to regulate fundraising for charities in all the UK jurisdictions. Principal legislation, in the Charities Acts 1992 (Part II) and 2011, the Charities and Trustee Investment (Scotland) Act 2005 and the Charities (Northern Ireland) Act 2008, is or will be supported by jurisdiction-specific supplementary regulations. However, progress has been slow, with Scotland the furthest advanced. As a result, only some of the updated law is in force at the date of preparation of this book. In other areas, the rules described below arise from considerably older legislation.

6.2.1 Public collections on behalf of charities – England and Wales

In England and Wales, public collections such as door-to-door and street collections of cash are largely subject to a local authority-based licensing regime. The regulatory regime largely flows from the House to House Collections Act 1939 and the Police, Factories etc. (Miscellaneous Provisions) Act 1916 and associated regulations. Although the Charities Act 2006 contains a modernised regime, it has not been brought into force. There are special provisions for nationwide collections by major charities, such as the Poppy Appeal for the Royal British Legion.

6.2.2 Fundraising regulations – England and Wales

The main current fundraising regulations relevant to England and Wales flow largely from Part II of the Charities Act 1992 and associated regulations. Some changes have been made by more recent statutory provisions, in particular, the requirements for statements to potential donors to be made by professional fundraisers and commercial participators fundraising for charities, have been 'beefed up' and clarified. Further reforms are still under discussion, as part of the review of charity law required by the Charities Act 2006.

Current regulations address fundraising by professional fundraisers and commercial participators.

A professional fundraiser is a person who carries on a fundraising business. That is a business carried on for gain that is wholly or primarily engaged in soliciting of otherwise procuring money or other property for charitable, benevolent or philanthropic purposes. In addition, any other person who, for reward, solicits money or other property for the benefit of a charitable institution is a professional fundraiser.

There are exceptions from the definition of professional fundraiser for:

- charitable institutions themselves;

- companies connected with charitable institutions (so most trading subsidiaries of charities are exempt, provided the charity, alone or with other charities, controls the voting rights at general meetings);

- officers, employees and trustees of charities, acting in those capacities;

- collectors in public charitable collections;

- people paid very small levels of remuneration (under £10 a day and £1,000 a year);

- people making broadcast appeals for charities (eg during TV or radio programmes).

A commercial participator is someone who carries on a non-fundraising business and, in the course of that business, carries out a promotional venture indicating that contributions will be made to or applied for the benefit of a 'charitable institution'.

A charitable institution is a charity or another institution established for charitable, benevolent or philanthropic purposes. Relevant ventures are advertising or sales campaigns and any other venture undertaken for a promotional purpose.

It should be noted that 'solicit' has a very wide meaning in this legislation:

> … solicit in any manner whatever whether expressly or impliedly or whether done:
>
> (i) by speaking directly to the person or persons to whom the solicitation is addressed (whether when in his presence or not), or
>
> (ii) by means of a statement published in any newspaper, film or radio or television programme,
>
> or otherwise, and references to a solicitation shall be construed accordingly

(section 58(6) of the Charities Act 1992 as amended).

Anyone responsible for receiving money or property solicited on behalf of a charitable institution is subject to the controls, even if that person did not personally make the solicitation. For example, if a third party is dealing with the receipts from an appeal made directly by the charity, that third party must comply with the regulatory requirements.

The statutory provisions:

- make it unlawful to solicit money and property on behalf of a charitable institution unless the relevant requirements have been met;

- require a written agreement between the charity and the regulated person (which must address particular matters);

- oblige the fundraiser to make specific statements to the public when making the solicitation; and

- impose criminal sanctions for non-compliance on the fundraiser (rather than the charity).

The precise information required in the statement to the public varies, depending on how the solicitation is made, whether the regulated fundraiser is a professional fundraiser or a commercial participator and whether more than one charitable institution is to benefit from the fundraising activities. Recent reforms have enhanced and clarified the detailed requirements.

6.2.3   Fundraising regulations – Scotland

Fundraising on behalf of charities or other 'benevolent bodies' in Scotland is subject to the requirements of:

- sections 79–83 of the Charities and Trustee Investment (Scotland) Act 2005; and

- the Charities and Benevolent Fundraising (Scotland) Regulations 2009.

These requirements extend to benevolent fundraisers, professional fundraisers and commercial participators. Further regulations will be made in due course in relation to public collections of cash and goods.

Note that the regulations do not only apply to fundraising for charities on the Scottish Charity Register. Fundraising for any charity or any 'benevolent body' is affected, ie a body set up for benevolent or philanthropic purposes.

A professional fundraiser is a person who carries on a fundraising business or who, in return for a financial reward, seeks money or other property for a benevolent body or for general charitable, benevolent or philanthropic purposes.

A commercial participator is an organisation carrying on a business, other than a fundraising business, that, in the course of the business, takes part in a promotional venture where some or all of the proceeds are to be given to benevolent bodies or used for charitable, benevolent or philanthropic purposes.

A benevolent fundraiser includes benevolent bodies and companies and extends to individuals:

- in management or control; or

- acting as employees or agents; or

- in some situations, acting as a volunteer.

Where the fundraising is undertaken by a professional fundraiser or a commercial participator, a written agreement addressing particular required areas must be entered into between that organisation and the charity.

There are detailed requirements about statements that must be made to the public in such fundraising initiatives, donor cancellation rights and other rules, such as record-keeping requirements and obligations regarding transfer of funds from the fundraiser to the beneficiary charity or other benevolent body.

The precise information that must be given to a potential donor varies, depending on whether the solicitation is oral or written and made by a benevolent fundraiser, a professional fundraiser or a commercial participator. It will include information about the intended beneficiary organisation(s) and the remuneration of the fundraiser.

Breaches of the legal requirements lead to criminal offences. Generally, the fundraiser will be liable, not the charity.

There are some valuable protections for charities, including rights to challenge and obtain prohibitions on unauthorised fundraising. Initially, this can be done by written request but, if that fails, application to the courts will be required.

6.2.4 Other legal rules that impact on fundraising

Many other legal rules can impact on fundraising ventures and initiatives. Obvious examples include regulations relating to broadcasting, telecommunications and e-commerce, consumer protection laws (particularly important for sales catalogues, shops, etc), travel bonding, tour operator and package holiday regulations, insurance and health and safety requirements (particularly important when an overseas 'challenge' event is being considered).

6.2.5   Risk assessment and management

Risk assessment and management are key considerations when planning fundraising ventures. This should include potential financial risks and also risks to reputation, through association with third parties considered unacceptable by donors and supporters, and risks arising from the fundraising activities themselves.

6.2.6   Role of the trustees

A charity's board should be careful to ensure it has identified, considered and adequately dealt with all the legal and practical implications of each major fundraising method the charity uses. Significant high risk ventures, including 'challenge' and 'endurance' style events, should be specifically authorised at board level.

6.2.7   Sources of guidance and useful reference points – charity fundraising

Fundraising Standards Board – the independent self-regulatory body for voluntary fundraising standards in the UK which aims to promote best practice and build confidence in fundraising (www.frsb.org.uk).

Institute of Fundraising – the professional body for UK fundraising which aims to promote the highest standards of fundraising practice as well as supporting fundraisers. It issues codes of practice and model agreements between charities and fundraisers (www.institute-of-fundraising.org.uk).

Public Fundraising Regulatory Association – a charity-led membership body which self-regulates all forms of face-to-face fundraising in public places, working with local authorities to ensure appropriate use of fundraising sites in public places. It has produced a useful *Face-to-Face Activity Code of Fundraising Practice* (www.pfra.org.uk).

The charity regulators also provide guidance on general trustees' responsibilities, fundraising and the correct safeguarding and use of charity funds and assets:

- Charity Commission, www.charity-commission.gov.uk;
- the OSCR, www.oscr.org.uk.

6.3   Investments

Charities' financial investments are a source of funding for those charities that hold such investments (many have no spare funds available to invest). A range of charity law requirements arise in the context of financial investments, in particular:

- trustees' duties (for further details, see Chapter 2);

- constitutional issues (especially with regard to the charity's investment powers, the trustees' powers and their exercise and the use of third party investment managers);

- statutory requirements and restrictions, especially those imposed on the trustees of unincorporated charities by the Trustee Act 2000.

The Trustee Act 2000 does not contain a definition of the word 'investment' but a wide interpretation is likely to be taken by a court (as it is by the Charity Commission).

6.3.1 Unincorporated charities – investment powers (England and Wales)

The Trustee Act 2000 provides trustees with a wide general statutory power of investment (section 3(1)):

> … a trustee may make any kind of investment that he could make if he were absolutely entitled to the assets of the trust.

This applies to the trustees of unincorporated charities, such as unincorporated trusts.

In relation to land, the Trustee Act 2000 provides a general power to acquire freehold or leasehold land in the UK. This is subject to any restrictions or exclusions in the individual charity's constitution.

6.3.2 Trustees' statutory duties – unincorporated charities

The trustees of unincorporated charities have a general statutory duty of care which requires them to 'exercise such care and skill as is reasonable in the circumstances' (section 1(1) of the Trustee Act 2000). This specifically applies when they exercise either the statutory general power of investment or any other power of investment, for example powers arising from the individual charity's constitution (Schedule 1 to the Trustee Act 2000).

The question of what is reasonable skill and care is a question of fact for determination in each case, taking into account all the circumstances. However, the Trustee Act 2000 states that specific regard must be had to:

- any special knowledge or experience the trustee holds himself out as having; and

- where the trustee acts in the course of a business or profession, any special knowledge or experience it is reasonable to expect of a person acting in the course of that business or profession.

The general statutory duty of care also applies in a number of other situations, listed in Schedule 1 to the Trustee Act 2000. They include when the trustees:

- have regard to the Standard Investment Criteria, to comply with section 4 of the Act;

- take appropriate investment advice to comply with section 5 of the Act;

- exercise the statutory power to acquire land, or any other powers in relation to land.

Some specialist trust lawyers believe that failure to comply with the statutory duty of care would render an investment unauthorised and constitute a breach of trust, so considerable care should be taken to comply.

6.3.3 Investment advice and the standard investment criteria (unincorporated charities)

Before exercising any power of investment (whether the statutory power or some other power, such as a power set out in the charity's constitution), the trustees must obtain and consider proper advice about the way in which that power should be exercised, having regard to the standard investment criteria. The same obligation to take advice applies when the trustees review investments and consider varying them.

The advice does not have to be confirmed in writing but it is clearly both good practice and a sensible protection for the trustees that there should be a written record.

The exception to these obligations is that trustees need not take advice if they reasonably conclude 'that in all the circumstances it is unnecessary or inappropriate to do so' (section 5(3) of the Trustee Act 2000). This exception should be used with care, taking into account all the circumstances, such as the size of the charity and the value of the sums under discussion, as well as the level of financial skills and knowledge amongst the trustees. If in any doubt about their competencies, the trustees would be wise to seek advice.

'Proper advice' is defined as the advice of a person who is reasonably believed 'to be qualified to give it by his ability in and practical experience of financial and other matters relating to the proposed investment' (section 5(4) of the Trustee Act 2000). The trustees must consider the advice but are not obliged to follow it. However to ignore the advice without good reason could be a breach of the general statutory duty of care.

The standard investment criteria are:

- the suitability to the charity of the type of investment being considered;
- the suitability of the particular investment as one of that type;
- the need for diversification of the charity's investments, as appropriate to the charity's circumstances.

Note that the duty to diversify applies to the exercise of any investment power, not just the general statutory power.

6.3.4 Investment management – general

The trustee board as a whole is responsible for the management of the charity's investments. The general trustees' duty of care applies.

In a larger charity, which has substantial investments, the board may establish an investment committee to advise the board on detailed aspects. The remit of such a committee needs to be clear and duly authorised by the main board. In particular, the extent to which the committee has authority to make decisions, including decisions about acquisitions and disposals of investments, should be clearly recorded. The board must still set and review the overall investment policy, as well as monitor performance against that policy.

Trustees may decide to use an investment manager to advise them, for example if they do not have sufficient expertise amongst the board members. It is essential to decide whether an adviser is to be appointed:

- to provide advice which the board uses to inform its decisions, in which case reference needs to be made to the board before any investment transactions occur; or
- to act as a discretionary investment manager, with delegated authority from the board to make investment decisions on its behalf and authorise transactions.

6.3.5   Investment management – unincorporated charities

The trustees of unincorporated charities are subject to the Trustee Act 2000 obligations, so there must be a written agreement with any investment manager who is appointed. That agreement must oblige the manager to observe the charity's investment policy. If discretionary management powers are being delegated, the agreement must also address the details of the relevant delegation. There are also restrictions that prevent appointments where there could be a conflict of interest and various other statutory limitations, for example the investment manager cannot normally include provisions in the agreement to reduce his or her duty of care.

The trustees' statutory duty of care applies to appointments of investment managers and any delegation of discretionary management authority to such managers. The board is also obliged to review both the suitability and the performance of investment managers regularly.

6.3.6   Investment – charitable companies (England and Wales)

The Trustee Act 2000 statutory investment powers and related statutory duties of trustees do not apply specifically to charitable companies. Whilst adopting an investment policy is therefore not a statutory requirement for a charitable company, it is certainly good practice.

In general, a charitable company is capable of investing funds, subject to any special trusts that exist over particular funds and subject to any specific limitations set out in its articles (or memorandum for older companies). The individual company's articles should also be checked in case they impose limitations or specific requirements on the trustees with regard to investment matters.

When making investment decisions and managing investments, including appointing and monitoring the performance of investment managers, the trustees of a charitable company are subject to the normal duties of trustees, especially in relation to risk and the proper application of charitable funds.

Although the more detailed Trustee Act 2000 duties, such as an obligation to review regularly the suitability and performance of an investment manager, do not specifically apply to the trustees of a charitable company, it is clearly wise to follow a similar process.

6.3.7 Investment (Scotland)

The relevant statutory provisions in the Charities and Trustee Investment (Scotland) Act 2005 apply to all legal forms of charities (unincorporated or incorporated).

6.3.8 Programme-related investment

Charities often invest their funds in order to further their charitable purposes, which is known as 'programme-related investment'. This might take the form of a loan to another organisation or guaranteeing another organisation's borrowing because that furthers the charity's own charitable purposes. Other mechanisms can include equity investment via a shareholding in a company and various forms of 'outcomes-based finance', where the funds are used to finance activities that deliver social benefits.

The Charity Commission does not consider programme-related investment to be subject to the legal framework for financial investment described earlier. However, it suggests there should be some expectation of financial return, compared to a grant which is a pure charitable gift, with no expectation of any return.

Trustees must ensure programme-related investment is made to further the charity's charitable purposes and that it is within both those purposes and the charity's powers. Care should be taken to observe any relevant restrictions in the individual charity's constitution. The board should also make the usual risk assessments and monitor performance against the public benefit objectives of the relevant programme.

6.3.9 Mixed motive investment

Some investments are 'mixed motive' with an expectation of some financial return alongside beneficial social outcomes. Investments by charities in outcomes-based programmes can sometimes be mixed motive, rather than purely programme-related investment. The Charity Commission expects trustees to be clear about the duality of purposes in such arrangements, and able to justify the use of charitable funds given the expected levels of both financial and social returns on the sum invested. As with all forms of investment, the arrangements must be in the charity's best interests and within its charitable purposes and its constitutional powers.

6.4   Borrowing and charges

A charity may borrow money to further its charitable purposes. Usually there will be an express borrowing power in the constitution, although a power to borrow in furtherance of the charitable purposes can be implied, provided the constitution does not expressly prohibit borrowing. A charitable company also benefits from the Companies Act 2006 presumption that a company may do anything lawful, unless its articles contain restrictions.

For all charities, *exercise* of borrowing powers must be in pursuit of the charitable purposes. The decision should be taken by the full board (not a committee), unless the borrowing is small scale and routine, such as ordering consumable office supplies on a credit basis. The usual trustees' duties apply when a board is considering borrowing money or granting security by means of a charge on any of the charity's assets.

A charity may give security for its borrowings provided it has the power to do so. That is likely to be an express constitutional power in the case of unincorporated charities. In addition, if their trustees hold or have held land, section 6(1) of the Trusts of Land and Appointment of Trustees Act 1996 gives the trustees full power to mortgage land (but that does not apply to land subject to the Universities and Colleges Estates Act 1925).

Charitable companies incorporated prior to the Companies Act 2006 are likely to have a specific borrowing power in their articles. Companies now benefit from their statutory power to do anything lawful (subject to any restrictions in the articles), so newer companies may not have specific empowering clauses.

The type of security and the nature of the assets charged depend on factors such as the loan terms and the lender's requirements, any relevant conditions or restrictions in the charity's constitution, advice given by the charity's professional advisers and the trustees' judgements regarding risk and the proper exercise of their powers in the particular circumstances.

6.4.1   Statutory restrictions on mortgages (sections 123 and 129 of the Charities Act 2011)

In addition to the general legal principles outlined above, if a charity intends to mortgage land held by, or on trust for, the charity it must comply with the requirements of the Charities Act 2011. These do not apply to exempt charities.

The provisions allow trustees to authorise the granting of a mortgage, without prior Charity Commission consent or a court order, provided they have first obtained, and duly considered, written advice from a person:

- whom they reasonably believe to be qualified by his or her ability in, and practical experience of, financial matters; and

- who has no financial interest in the making of the loan (or grant) to be secured.

The advice must address certain matters:

1. whether the grant or loan is necessary in order for the trustees to pursue a particular course of action in connection with which they are seeking the loan; and

2. whether the loan or grant terms are reasonable, having regard to the status of the charity as a prospective borrower (or grant recipient); and

   (a) the charity's ability to repay the relevant sum, on the proposed terms; or, in the case of any other obligation

   (b) whether it is reasonable for the trustees to undertake to discharge the obligation, having regard to the charity's purposes.

The trustees may decide that several different specialist advisers should be engaged, in order to provide the wide range of advice required. Although the statutory provisions do not prevent reliance on a member of staff for relevant advice, it is normally prudent to seek independent professional advice (not least to ensure there is professional indemnity insurance in place should the advice prove to be negligent).

6.5   Charities – social enterprise and trading

A charity can trade in direct pursuit of its charitable purposes. This is known as 'primary purpose trading'. Examples of primary purpose trading might include:

- a charitable theatre, with a charitable purpose to educate the public in the performing arts, selling seats for performances;

- an educational charity charging for providing educational materials to teachers and schools.

Such trading is perfectly acceptable from a charity law perspective, subject to the terms of the individual charity's constitution and the normal charity rules and principles such as risk management, the correct use of charitable assets and the rules on public benefit. The latter are especially important with regard to charges potentially inhibiting access to benefits for those less able, or unable, to afford the charges.

Primary purpose trading needs to be distinguished from commercial trading activities to raise funds (ie fundraising trading). Even though the funds are used for the charitable purposes, this is 'non-primary purpose trading' (it is not activities being done in direct pursuit of the charitable purposes in order to provide the charitable public benefit). Such fundraising trading by the charity itself must be treated with some caution. If undertaken on a larger scale, or to the detriment of the direct charitable activities, it might incur a tax charge and/or potentially prejudice the charity's charitable status. The use of a trading subsidiary may therefore be either desirable or necessary.

6.5.1   Social enterprise

Social enterprise essentially involves carrying out business activities with the objective of achieving some wider social benefit whilst also creating surplus funds to sustain the activities. This is sometime described as 'profit with a purpose'.

The term 'social enterprise' has no strict legal meaning. In practice, there is a very wide spectrum of organisations and activities that might be considered to be engaging in social enterprise – from the purely philanthropic and charitable to significant commercial organisations and activities, where some of the profits are paid out to the business owners or third party investors.

Charities engage with social enterprise in a variety of ways. Some use it as the means of carrying out their charitable activities, for instance providing chargeable services such as window cleaning or garden maintenance in order to develop the work and life skills of the beneficiaries, with a view to re-integrating them into society and helping them gain independent employment. Others use it as a form of fundraising trading or for mixed purposes. It is important to analyse the underlying purposes and the implications of any activities regarded by the charity as 'social enterprise'. The activities must be structured correctly, so they do not pose unacceptable risks to the charity's charitable funds and assets, have unexpected taxation consequences or put charitable status at risk. Professional advice should be taken and a trading subsidiary may be desirable or necessary.

6.5.2 Charity shops

The sale of donated second hand items, provided by donors as a pure gift, is treated as conversion of a donation into cash. HM Revenue & Customs will not seek to tax the funds raised. A charity may therefore choose to operate this kind of traditional charity shop operation directly, rather than through a trading company.

' If new goods are to be sold or the charity intends to operate as an agent for donors, selling their goods before inviting them to choose to donate the sum raised back to the charity, with Gift Aid, matters are significantly more complex in terms of charity law and regulation, as well as tax. Considerable care should be taken to structure and document such activities correctly and professional advice is strongly recommended. A trading subsidiary may be needed.

6.5.3 Trustees' responsibilities

The trustees must ensure the charity pursues its charitable purposes and that its activities and the use of its funds and assets are directed to that end. They must make some careful judgements about the types of trading a charity is undertaking (including anything regarded as 'social enterprise') and how those can properly be carried out. The analysis should include whether the activities can or should be undertaken directly by the charity itself, or whether a trading subsidiary should be used.

It is important to check and observe any permanent trading restrictions in the charity's constitution. The trustees have a duty to ensure the charity operates within its constitutional powers.

The board has overall responsibility for the correct management of all the charity's trading activities. In discharging this, the board must particularly consider how the activities fit with the charity's current strategy and address risk management, including risk of loss or misapplication of charitable funds and potential reputational damage. Good performance management is essential. This should include setting SMART (specific, measurable, achievable, realistic, time-bound) targets and monitoring performance against these, as well as regular review of all trading activities.

The board should seek to reduce the exposure to tax of the funds generated, so far as lawful and practicable, whilst ensuring solvency and retaining sufficient working capital.

The trustees are responsible for compliance with relevant public reporting and accounting obligations, in relation to all types of trading.

Trading is a complex area for charities, in which the judgements required may be finely balanced. Professional advice is likely to be essential.

6.5.4   The charity regulators' perspective

The charity regulators expect trustees to exercise appropriate care and be mindful of their duties and responsibilities when addressing any trading activities (including duties with regard to investments). The Charity Commission has issued specific guidance *Trustees, trading and tax – How charities may lawfully trade* (see www.charitycommission.gov.uk).

This concentrates on when and how the Commission considers charities may lawfully trade to raise funds (rather than addressing primary purpose trading, ie trading to carry out the charitable purposes). It emphasises that the interests of the charity are paramount and sets out some key principles. The guidance states that, due to the complexities of the law and the potential scale of adverse consequences if mistakes are made, trustees should obtain professional advice in relation to any substantial trading activities.

The OSCR's *Guidance for Charity Trustees, 'acting with care and diligence'* (see www.oscr.org.uk) should be considered in the context of charities on the Scottish Charity Register.

6.5.5   Other legal rules that impact on trading

Potentially, a wide range of other legal rules impact on a charity's trading activities. Depending on the mix of business activities and how these are being undertaken, areas of potential relevance include (but are not limited to):

* contract law;
* competition law;
* data protection;
* financial services legislation;
* advertising regulations;
* consumer protection and consumer safety legislation;
* e-commerce regulations/distance selling regulations/direct marketing regulations;
* intellectual property law (trademarks, patents, copyright, domain names, etc);
* food and hygiene regulations, alcohol licensing and other public licensing requirements.

6.5.6 Public benefit dimension

Charities are obliged to operate for the public benefit and must seek to provide benefit that is appropriate to their charitable purposes (as set out in their individual constitutions). The trustees must therefore consider the potentially restrictive effect of any fees charged for charitable services or facilities (fees charged in the context of primary purpose trading). They need to have a reasonable basis for making charges and for setting the levels of those charges. Wherever possible, the trustees should seek ways to widen access to charitable benefits for people less able to afford fees.

Any private benefit arising from a charity's activities should be purely incidental to the public benefit provided (eg a necessary and minor by-product of the charitable services or facilities provided by the charity to its beneficiaries or the public at large). Care should be taken to ensure significant private benefits and commercial benefits do not arise and potential conflicts of interest must be identified and actively managed. Significant failures in such areas could, at worst, amount to a breach of trustees' duties or even put charitable status at risk.

6.6 Taxation – trading

Tax and VAT issues relating to trading are potentially complex and high-risk areas in relation to the trading activities of charities and not-for profits. It is often wrongly assumed that such organisations are blanket exempt from VAT (which they are not). It is also sometimes wrongly assumed that because the underlying nature of such organisations is non-commercial, any surplus funds generated by trading activities would not be taxable. In fact, the key issue is whether an exemption from tax applies to the income in the particular situation. If not, a tax charge may arise. Careful analysis of all trading activities, with suitable professional advice, is essential to ensure tax and VAT issues are understood and dealt with correctly.

6.6.1 Taxation of trading income – charity

Profits arising from *primary purpose* trading by a charity are usually exempt from tax, provided relevant statutory criteria are met (Income Tax Act 2007/Corporation Tax Act 2010), they include:

- the activity is to further that charity's charitable purposes (medical services provided by a charitable hospital, residential care provided by a charitable care home, etc); or

- the trade is carried out mainly by the beneficiaries (a workshop that employs people with disabilities to produce goods that are sold to the public).

In addition, the profits must be applied by the charity to further its own charitable activities.

Income 'ancillary' to the charitable activities is also generally exempt from tax (a bar open only to those attending performances in a charitable theatre or exhibitions in a charitable art gallery). However, if the facilities are made available to the public at large, the income will be taxable.

Profits arising from *non-primary purpose* trading (ie commercial trading aimed at raising funds, such as Christmas card sales, affinity credit cards, etc) are taxable. There is *small scale (de minimis)* exemption (section 46 of the Finance Act 2000, in relation to corporation tax, sections 526 and 528 of the Income Taxes Act 2007, in relation to income tax). The exemption will only apply:

- if the turnover from all the charity's non-exempt trading activities is within the annual turnover limit of £5,000; or

- if the annual turnover is above £5,000, to 25% of the charity's total incoming resources, up to a maximum of £50,000.

'Total incoming resources' means the charity's total receipts from all sources, including grants, investment income, donations and trading income.

The Charity Commission is content that commercial trading within these limits does not prejudice the charitable status, not least because the level of risk to charitable resources is small.

6.6.2 Taxation of trading income – subsidiary

A trading subsidiary is subject to tax on its retained profits, under normal corporation tax rules. However, the surplus funds it gives to its parent charity can be given tax free as a corporate Gift Aid donation. This must be made within 9 months of the financial year end (a special time limit for wholly owned subsidiaries). All the other usual corporate Gift Aid rules and record-keeping requirements apply.

6.7 Rate relief

Where a charity occupies premises and uses them for its charitable purposes, it is entitled to 80% mandatory rate relief from non-domestic rates and can also be considered for a discretionary additional 20% relief. Primary purpose trading (in pursuit of the charitable purposes) and selling donated goods do not prejudice this. Commercial trading to raise funds might do so (especially if the trading becomes substantial). The relief does not apply to commercial trading by a trading subsidiary.

The key conditions for the relief are (section 47(2) of the Local Government Finance Act 1988):

- the charity is the ratepayer for the premises (or its trustees, in the case of an unincorporated charity); and

- the property is used 'wholly or mainly' for charitable purposes.

7 Practical Operation

This chapter indicates important areas likely to be most relevant in the practical operation of a charity or civil society organisation.

7.1 Land transactions

Trustees have general responsibility for the protection and proper use of all the charity's resources. All assets must be safeguarded against loss or damage and correctly applied for the charity's charitable purposes. Particular responsibilities (acquisition and disposal) and rights arise in relation to land, as well as granting security over land. Particular caution is required in relation to borrowing funds and using charitable assets as security for borrowing, as this potentially exposes assets to risk of loss.

If the charity is unincorporated, title to land must be held in the names of the individual trustees (or some other custodian) as the charity does not have its own legal capacity. Incorporated charities may acquire title in their own right.

Land-related matters are complex areas, which involve significant potential risks to the charity and its trustees. Beyond the basic charity law restrictions and requirements, there are further specific statutory controls relevant to land transactions, for example:

- requirements for particular statements and certifications in documents relating to the conveyance, transfer, lease or other disposal of land by or in trust for a charity (sections 117, 122 and 123 of the Charities Act 2011 and relevant land registration rules);

- restrictions on, and special procedures in relation to, disposing of, or mortgaging, charity land (Part 7 of the Charities Act 2011) (for details regarding mortgaging charity land, see Chapter 6);

- additional restrictions and obligations where any proposed disposal is to a 'connected person' (sections 117 and 118 of the Charities Act 2011); and

- investment requirements under the Trustee Act 2000 (these are relevant to unincorporated charities in England and Wales).

Professional advice should be taken by the trustees when considering all major decisions and transactions relating to land. Such matters should also be dealt with by the full trustee board (not a sub-committee).

7.1.1   Disposals of land – general

Few disposals of land now require formal Charity Commission consent (as was once the case). Rather, most are subject to the requirements of the Charities Act 2011 (see Part 7 of the Act) unless one of the specified exemptions applies or the disposal falls into another special category (such as a disposal to other charities in order to pursue the disposing charity's charitable purposes).

Exempt charities are not obliged to follow the full disposal procedures but must include certain statements in the contract, transfer or lease.

A disposal by an unincorporated charity to vest the title in a new trustee, alongside the existing trustees, is not a sale, lease or real disposal, but rather a necessary legal formality. Such a disposal is not subject to the normal restrictions and requirements on disposal of charity land.

Other special types of disposal where the full statutory obligations do not apply are listed below. Note that special statements must be made in the relevant documents and, in the case of short leases, particular advice must be obtained and considered by the trustees before the disposal is made. The relevant types of disposal are:

- a disposal to another charity, at less than best price, within the trusts of the disposing charity (ie in order to pursue the disposing charity's charitable purposes);

- a lease to a beneficiary, under the charity's trusts, at less than best price, with the intention the occupation will pursue the charity's charitable purposes;

- a disposal authorised by statute or by a scheme;

- a disposal authorised under the Universities and College Estates Act 1925;

- a lease of 7 years or less (not granted wholly or partly in consideration of a fine).

7.1.2 Disposals regulated by section 117 of the Charities Act 2011

For other disposals of land held by or in trust for a charity, the full statutory requirements are likely to be compulsory. For these purposes a disposal (described in the Charities Act 2011 as a 'disposition') includes:

- the conveyance or transfer of land;

- a lease of more than 7 years; and

- other disposals.

In summary, the requirements for such disposals are as follows:

1. The trustees must first obtain a written report from a qualified surveyor (regulations specify the qualifications required). The report must address a range of specified matters and that person must be instructed by the trustees and act exclusively for the charity.

2. The proposed disposal must be publicly advertised in the manner recommended by the surveyor (unless the surveyor advises that advertising would not be in the charity's best interests).

3. Before formally deciding to make the disposal, the full trustee board (not a sub-committee) must consider the advice received in the report and be satisfied that the proposed disposal terms are the best that can reasonably be obtained for the charity.

Required statements must be included in the contract and conveyance or transfer or lease. The precise wording varies according to the specific situation.

7.1.3 Disposals where land is held for stipulated purposes

If the land to be disposed of is subject to trusts which stipulate that it is to be used for the charity's purposes in general, or for particular purposes within those overall purposes, for example to be used as an almshouse, the procedures summarised at para 7.1.2 are supplemented by a specific public advertisement obligation (section 121 of the Charities Act 2011). The public notice must invite representations to be made to the trustees, within a stated time limit (not less than a month from the notice date). If any representations are made, the trustees must consider these before taking a decision about the proposed disposal.

These advertising requirements do not apply if:

- the disposal is made with a view to acquiring replacement property to be used for the same purposes; or

- the disposal is a lease for no longer than 2 years (and not granted wholly or partly in consideration of a fine); or

- the Charity Commission gives a direction that the requirements will not apply because that is in the charity's best interests.

Note that land held under particular trusts may be 'functional endowment', part of the charity's inalienable capital assets and required to be retained and used for specific charitable activities (a school, an almshouse, etc). In such relatively rare instances, additional legal restrictions apply. In such cases specialist advice should be taken, as it may be necessary to obtain external authority for a disposal (such as formal consent from the Charity Commission, or a scheme approved by the Commission and authorised by the court).

7.1.4   Disposals to 'connected persons' (sections 117(1) and (2) and 118 of the Charities Act 2011)

The general requirements that permit disposals under the Charities Act 2011 procedures summarised above do *not* apply to proposed disposals to 'connected persons'. Such disposals will require Charity Commission consent (unless they fall within the limited exceptions discussed at para 7.1.1).

The Charities Act 2011 defines connected persons as:

(a)   a charity trustee of or for the charity;

(b)   a person who is the donor of the land to the charity;

(c)   a child, parent, grandchild, grandparent, brother or sister of such a trustee or donor;

(d)   an officer, agent or employee of the charity;

(e)   the spouse or civil partner of anyone in (a)–(d) above;

(f)   a person carrying on business in partnership with anyone in (a)–(e) above;

7.2   Contracts

A contract is a legally enforceable agreement, made between two or more parties that have legal capacity to enter into the contract (for example, limited companies or adult individuals). It requires certain key legal elements, in particular an offer, an acceptance of that offer and adequate valuable consideration.

Since a party to a contract must have legal identity and capacity, it is important to check whether the charity:

- itself exists as a separate legal entity; and

- has the power to enter into the proposed contract.

A separate, but equally important, matter to check is the authority of the individual(s) dealing with the matter on the charity's behalf.

An unincorporated charity has no independent legal identity, so contracts must be entered into by its individual trustees, with potential exposure to personal liability. Subject to that point, in general, charities can enter into contracts provided:

- the contract furthers the charity's charitable purposes;

- the charity has the power to enter into the particular contract (usually flowing from the charity's own constitution);

- any additional legal requirements are followed (eg Charities Act 2011 requirements with regard to contracts for the disposal or mortgage of land held by or on trust for a charity);

- the trustees authorise the terms of the contract (directly or via properly delegated authority to the charity's staff);

- the signatories to the contract, if it is in writing, are properly authorised to sign on the charity's behalf.

A contract may, but generally does not have to, be in writing. Provided the essential legal elements of a contract are present, an organisation will be legally committed to, bound by, and liable in respect of, any agreement that amounts to a contract. So a binding legal contract might be purely oral, or it may be partially evidenced by documents (this can include email as well as traditional paper-based communications), or it may be fully documented in a formal written contract.

It is clearly good practice for all major contracts to be in writing and most contracts relating to land must be written, due to land law requirements. Small, routine contracts, relating to day-to-day matters such as repeat stationery orders, are often placed with a supplier by phone, email or online. Whilst in such situations there will not be a full written contract, some record of it should be made and retained by the charity as evidence of its rights and commitments in the matter. It is also important to check suppliers' standard terms and conditions.

Individuals negotiating and agreeing a contract on behalf of a charity should be properly authorised to do so. This may a be a general delegated authority, such as the authority a chief executive has been given under the terms of his or her job role, contract of employment and the charity's internal financial controls. In other situations it may be a specific authority, given by the board to those individuals in the particular situation. Careful documentation of authority levels, and the details of the authority delegated (whether it is general or specific), is important. Minutes of relevant board meetings should be carefully drafted in this respect.

Major contractual commitments and contracts relating to land should normally be authorised by the full board before the charity finally commits to them.

7.2.1 Contract party

Whilst the name in which the contract is entered into ought to be a simple matter to deal with correctly, it is surprisingly common for potentially significant errors to occur. Often this is because of failure to check the details of the charity or misunderstanding of its legal nature. An unincorporated charity does not have its own legal capacity, so it cannot enter into a contract in its own right and its own name. Rather individuals, such as the trustees, must enter into the contract in their personal names and capacities.

The consequences of errors regarding the contracting parties can be substantial and might include unexpected personal liability for trustees or doubts about the charity's rights and their validity. There may also be difficulties in enforcing the terms of the contract in favour of the charity. Third parties are usually protected by law from disadvantage, provided they acted in good faith.

7.2.2 *Ultra vires*

A charity must not enter a contract which is *ultra vires* (ie beyond its powers). For example, if the charity's objects limit it to assisting young people aged 18 or under, it does not have lawful capacity to provide charitable services to the general adult population. It is essential to check the constitution carefully to ensure there are adequate powers for the charity to enter into the proposed contract and that no relevant constraints or prohibitions apply.

Likewise, the trustees must not act beyond their powers in relation to a contract to be made by, or on behalf of, the charity. Any other individuals acting for the charity in contractual matters must have sufficient authority to do so. It is therefore important to check the constitution when considering who can be given delegated authority in matters of contract (eg the charity's chief executive and senior managers or committees of the board of trustees).

If an *ultra vires* arrangement *beyond the powers of the charity* is made, the trustees risk personal liability for breach of trust. In addition, the charity can recover losses from its trustees. The charity regulators might also intervene if charitable assets were at risk.

If individuals go beyond their powers and authority, but the matter is still within the lawful powers of the charity, there may be potential personal liability risks to the relevant unauthorised individuals. The trustees could also be at risk of liability for breach of trust.

Generally, third parties are protected in such situations, although in the case of charitable companies the protection is more limited than would be the case for third parties dealing with commercial companies. The third party will generally be protected if they gave full consideration and did not know the action was *ultra vires*, or if they did not know they were dealing with a charity. Where an interest in property is involved, and that passes on to a subsequent further third party, that ultimate purchaser will not normally be prejudiced, provided they gave full consideration and did not have actual notice of the earlier invalidity.

The general power, for company members to ratify invalid transactions involving directors and persons associated with directors, does not apply to a charitable company. Such ratification is only possible if the Charity Commission gives specific prior consent (see section 42 of the Companies Act 2006).

7.3 Employment

Some charities and not-for-profit organisations employ paid staff. It is important to be clear whether or not an individual has employment status or some other relationship to the charity, such as a 'worker' contractor or an independent 'non-worker' contractor or a volunteer. If an individual's status is unclear it would be wise to take legal advice, and subsequent appropriate steps, to clarify that individual's position in relation to the organisation.

The following comments point out some general principles. Employment law is a complex and potentially high risk area in which specialist advice should be taken.

Employees have significant basic statutory rights and entitlements, including:

- not to be unfairly dismissed (this applies after the relevant qualifying period has been worked);

- not to be discriminated against;

- holiday pay;

- trade union membership;

- statutory minimum wage.

Other rights largely depend on their terms and conditions of employment and any specific contract of employment they have entered into with the employer.

For a dismissal to be fair the reason for it (or the principal reason, if there is more than one reason) must be a *fair reason* and the employer must follow a *fair process* before making the decision to dismiss.

The law recognises these as *potentially* fair reasons for dismissal:

- redundancy;

- capability;

- conduct;

- breach of a statutory duty;

- some other substantial reason that justifies dismissal of that employee.

Employees must work in return for their pay, obey reasonable instructions, act in their employer's best interests and abide by the terms of their contract of employment (which is likely to include standard terms and conditions that the employer requires of all its employees).

It is vital that an employer complies with requirements regarding documentation that an employee is entitled to have (at the most basic level, this is at least a 'written statement of particulars of employment'). It is also important that the employer keeps adequate records relating to employees and employment matters. Records will address areas such as:

- a written statement of particulars of employment or a written contract for each employee;

- national insurance and PAYE records;

- holiday and sickness absence records;

- written evidence of any changes to standard terms and conditions for all staff or changes to individual contracts of employment.

Other areas of particular importance in the context of employment of staff by charities include:

- equality law (Equalities Act 2010);

- safeguarding legislation and the vetting and barring scheme (or equivalents in Scotland, Wales and Northern Ireland);

- work permit regulations;

- pensions law and regulation;

- TUPE (the Transfer of Undertakings (Protection of Employment) Regulations 2006 (SI 2006/246)).

Pensions and TUPE are especially relevant, and potentially problematic, in relation to mergers and restructuring of charities and other civil society organisations.

General information and useful resources regarding employers and their employees are available from:

- ACAS, www.acas.org.uk;

- Business Link, www.businesslink.gov.uk;

- the employment section of the Direct Government website, www.direct.gov.uk/en/Employment.

7.4 Data protection

Gathering, holding and use of information that is 'personal data' is subject to the requirements of the Data Protection Act 1998, and supplementary legislation. The requirements of the Act extend to data held in paper and electronic form (or any combination) and obligations are imposed on both 'data controllers' and 'data processors'. Charities and other not-for-profit organisations are subject to these requirements and should ensure they have appropriate procedures and follow correct practice in relation to data.

Data that relates to a living individual and allows identification of that individual (via that data alone, or that data used in conjunction with other data or information the data controller possesses or is likely to possess) amounts to 'personal data'.

Additional regulations apply in relation to 'sensitive personal data', which includes information such as an individual's:

- racial or ethnic origin;

- physical health or sexual life;

- religious beliefs;

- trade union affiliation;

- criminal record (including any allegation of the commission of an offence).

The law places particular obligations on those who control data. A 'data controller' is someone who, either alone or jointly with others, directs how and why personal data are to be processed. Data controllers have specific direct obligations under the legislation. These include obligations to protect and use properly the data they have gathered on individuals.

A data controller must comply with the eight data protection principles:

1. Personal data must be processed fairly and lawfully.

2. Data should be obtained only for one or more stated and lawful purposes and must not be processed in a way incompatible with those purposes.

3. Data must be adequate, relevant and not excessive in relation to the purposes for which it is processed.

4. Data should be accurate and, where necessary, up to date.

5. Data must not be kept for longer than is necessary for the purposes for which it is processed.

6. Data must be processed in accordance with the rights of data subjects.

7. The data controller must take appropriate technical and organisational measures to protect against unauthorised or unlawful processing of data, and against accidental loss or destruction of, or damage to, the data.

8. Data must not be transferred to any country or territory outside the European Economic Area unless that country or territory ensures an adequate level of protection for the rights and freedoms of data subjects, in relation to the processing of personal data.

Individuals who are the 'data subjects' have legal rights to know that data is being gathered about them and why and, to some extent, to have access to the data to ensure its accuracy.

The Data Protection Act 1998 also includes provisions relevant to 'data processors', ie anyone (other than an employee of a data controller) who processes data on behalf of, and at the direction of, a data controller (eg a fulfilment house). Although the legislation does not impose direct obligations on data processors, it requires data controllers to ensure there is a signed written contract between controller and processor, which must include particular obligations on the processor. This is important for charities that engage contractors in communicating with individuals on behalf of the charity (fundraising appeals, etc).

'Processing' is very widely defined and includes obtaining, recording, organising, using, disclosing, deleting and simply holding data. Essentially, anything done with data is likely to amount to 'processing'.

The Information Commissioner has enforcement powers and there is a penalty regime for non-compliance with the data protection legislation (including criminal offences).

The Information Commissioner's Office provides useful information and resources regarding data protection law and practice (www.ico.gov.uk).

7.5   Intellectual property

Intellectual property includes legal rights in a range of matters, such as trademarks, names, logos, domain names, designs, books and writings, drawings, images, music, sounds, databases and much else. Whilst the relevant property is often intangible, rather than physical, the rights in relation to it are binding and enforceable against third parties, and the law provides various mechanisms to protect those rights and enable an owner whose rights are at risk to take protective action, as well as providing redress for actual infringements. Charities are often at best naïve in relation to such matters, failing to recognise and protect their own rights and the value of those rights to the charity, or even ignoring the rights of others (eg by using images over which a third party has rights without first obtaining appropriate permission).

It is important to identify what intellectual property rights a charity has and to manage and protect those rights. The charity should therefore always address intellectual property issues when material is being created for it by individuals, whether unpaid volunteers or third party contractors. Particular care should be taken with regard to the creation of logos or material for websites, material for publications and communications (whether paper-based or electronic), and the creation or use of images (of any type, including photographic images, video and film images, etc). Ideally, full rights should be reserved to the charity, so that it has ownership in relation to all future use of the relevant material. This should be documented in writing, through legally enforceable assignment or licensing as appropriate.

When considering allowing a third party to make use of intellectual property owned by the charity, it is important to consider:

- whether any other party has rights in relation to the material and should be consulted for consent;

- an appropriate payment to the charity (unless the use is a charitable use, in direct pursuit of the charity's charitable purposes);

- what tax and VAT implications there may be in relation to that payment;

- what legal documentation should be put in place (usually some form of contract);

- the limitations and protections that should be included (not only to clarify permitted uses but also to protect the charity's rights and its reputation).

7.5.1 Trademarks

A trademark identifies goods or services. Both the charity itself and its trading subsidiary may be able to protect certain of their legal rights through trademark registration (especially in relation to names and logos – which are key aspects of their 'brands'). Trademark registration under UK law is regulated by the Trade Marks Act 1994. Under section 1(1) a trademark is any sign which:

1.   can be represented graphically; and

2.   distinguishes particular goods or services of one party from those of another party.

Registration of a trademark gives the owner of the mark exclusive rights to use it in connection with the goods or services for which it is registered. There are 43 different classes of goods and services in respect of which a UK trademark can exist. Note that it is not necessary for a mark owner to sell goods or services commercially in order to seek a trademark registration. However, there are a number of other conditions to meet, such as a name being distinctive and not merely descriptive of the goods or services.

UK trademark registration is dealt with by the UK Intellectual Property Office (IPO) (which is part of the Patent Office). The IPO provides useful guidance and information on its website (www.ipo.gov.uk).

It is also possible to register a Community Trademark under EU law, via the Office for Harmonisation of the European Union. Specific conditions must be met, including the distinctiveness of the relevant mark. Community Trademark registration provides protection for the mark owner in the UK and in the other countries of the EU, however costs of registration are considerably higher than in the UK.

7.5.2 Domain name registration

A domain name is the means by which websites and web pages are located and unique email addresses located when using electronic internet communications. It often appears in an organisation's email address and website address. In the UK, registration of domain names (eg .org.uk) is managed by Nominet, which is the registrar of 'uk' domain names (see www.nominet.org.uk).

7.6 Campaigning and political activities

An organisation with political purposes is not capable of being a charity in law, as charities must have exclusively charitable purposes, for the public benefit. The Charity Commission considers that any purpose directed at furthering the interests of a political party, or intended to secure or oppose a change in the law or in policy or political decisions, in England and Wales or overseas, is a political purpose.

However, provided appropriate activities are chosen and undertaken in genuine pursuit of the individual charity's purposes, the regulator recognises that a charity may properly campaign and undertake some political activities (but not party political activities). Such campaigning must not become the charity's only activity. Likewise, trustees should not allow the entire resources of the charity to become devoted to political activities. Staying true to the fundamental charitable purpose is essential.

Changes to law, policy or political decisions may be the subject of campaigning by charities, provided the change would further the relevant charitable purposes. All the general legal regulations and standards in relation to such campaigning should be properly observed, for example in relation to public order and advertising.

The independence of the charity must always be safeguarded and its trustees should also be mindful of the charity's reputation and general good standing. Trustees should also ensure the charity is not hijacked by the personal political views of some of its trustees or staff, members or volunteers. Likewise, the trustees should protect the charity from being used for a political party's purposes.

Political activities should be balanced, with a clear and justifiable link to the charitable purposes. A charity must not give support or funding to a specific political party, nor to an individual candidate or politician. Particular care should be taken in these areas during election periods.

A charity must always observe the limitations in its own constitution, which may be more restrictive than the limits of the general law that have been summarised above.

Charity trustees and professional advisers assisting charities should take careful note of the Charity Commission's published guidance on these matters, *Speaking Out: Guidance on Campaigning and Political Activity by Charities* (CC9) (see www.charitycommission.gov.uk).

7.6.1 Campaigning and political activities – community interest companies

CICs are not permitted to carry out various party political or political campaigning activities. The Community Interest Company Regulations (SI 2005/1788) (see Part 2) specify that an organisation carrying out any of the following is not to be treated as carrying out activities for the community (and therefore may not be registered as a CIC):

1. promoting or opposing legal change (in Britain or elsewhere);

2. promoting or opposing the policy of government or any public authority;

3. providing financial or other support for a political party or political campaigning organisation;

4. influencing voters in relation to an election or referendum;

5. being a political party;

6. being a political campaigning organisation;

7. being a subsidiary of a political party or a political campaigning organisation.

There is an exception for any of items 1–4 if the activity can reasonably be regarded as incidental to other community benefit activities which are not within a prohibited category.

7.7 Monitoring, evaluation and quality

Charities need to monitor and evaluate what they do, and consider appropriate ways to ensure and verify the quality of their services and activities. Doing so should help them:

*   retain their focus on their charitable purposes;

*   deliver appropriate charitable outcomes (and therefore appropriate charitable public benefit);

- put their beneficiaries at the forefront of their activities;

- make best use of their limited resources;

- secure the sustainable future of their activities;

- have good strategic management and effective planning for the future;

- report openly and honestly, as part of their wider public accountability.

Monitoring is focused on measuring and interpreting information. Data is collected and considered to help inform decision-making and to ensure current policies and procedures are being followed and are having their intended effect. This is an important activity within the governance and management of the charity. From the trustees' perspective, appropriate monitoring mechanisms are vital in both risk management and in their overall custodianship of the charity and its assets.

Evaluation is more typically the periodic assessment of either the organisation as whole or some aspect of the organisation and its activities. Such an exercise is generally set against a wider context, such as strategic objectives and targets or expected future developments and changes amongst beneficiaries and their needs, or wider society.

Quality assurance activities should focus on the quality of activities undertaken and also of their outcomes (ie the results, sometimes called 'impacts'). Externally accredited quality assurance systems may be useful in large charities but are likely to be impractical and perhaps too complex and costly for most charities (the majority of charities are quite small in terms of income, personnel (paid and/or volunteer) and other resources).

Impact assessment, that is establishing and demonstrating the effect that a charity's activities have had, is an increasingly important matter for charities. This should be focused on the charitable benefit provided, through the activities the charity undertakes in pursuit of its charitable purposes. So it should certainly not be regarded as a separate or different matter from public reporting of the charitable public benefit provided by the charity.

7.8   Controls and risk management

Every charity or other civil society organisation needs suitable controls and appropriate risk management in place. These need to be appropriate to the nature of the organisation and its activities and they must be effective – achieving the necessary levels of assurance and preventing serious harm occurring to the organisation. The trustee board should take responsibility for deciding the areas where controls and risk management procedures are needed and focusing efforts on the most important of those identified areas. Examples of where the greatest attention is likely to be needed include:

- safeguarding children and vulnerable beneficiaries;

- health and safety;

- budgets, costs and expenditure;

- financial performance, cash flow and solvency;

- anti-fraud measures and other deterrents to major criminal risks (such as theft, bribery and money laundering);

- the security and the correct application of funds and assets.

7.8.1   Financial controls

The Charity Commission suggests that the key aims of internal financial controls are:

- to protect the charity's assets;

- to identify and manage the risk of loss, waste, theft or fraud;

- to ensure the financial reporting is robust and of sufficient quality; and

- to ensure that the trustees comply with charity law and regulation relating to finance.

It is essential for the trustees to have a thorough knowledge and an accurate understanding of the charity's finances. If a charity is to make a real impact, providing charitable outcomes for the public benefit, its trustees need to ensure the funds, assets and all other resources are correctly identified and properly used. Funds must be spent effectively and the financial affairs need to be well managed. There is also a need to look to the future, ensuring the continued viability of the charity itself and the sustainability of its charitable activities. Appropriate financial controls need to be in place for all of these reasons.

In addition, such controls are part of the charity's risk management, particularly in reducing the risk and potential harmful impact of fraud, theft, loss, misappropriation of funds and other misuse or abuse of the charity's funds and assets. Anti-bribery financial safeguards will also be particularly relevant to many charities because of the bribery risks of their activities, or the particular risks arising from where and how those activities are carried out. Whilst controls cannot completely eliminate any of these risks, effective controls can and should significantly reduce them.

The controls chosen must be appropriate to the charity's size, the complexity and nature of its activities and the areas of key risk for that particular charity in its particular situation. They must also be effective and the board should ensure that effectiveness is reviewed periodically (the Charity Commission suggests this should be done annually). Much of this work may be able to be dealt with by the charity's board, staff and volunteers. However, some external independent professional scrutiny of the charity's systems and procedures, and periodic external advice about their appropriateness and effectiveness, is often an added safeguard and a reassurance to the board and the external stakeholders (including members, donors and other funders).

Developing and maintaining a culture of shared responsibility for good practice, and for adhering to appropriate financial controls and practices, embedded throughout the organisation, is just as important as establishing the controls and practices in the first place. These are matters to be taken seriously by all trustees, staff and volunteers and should not be regarded as the responsibility of simply a few.

7.8.2   External scrutiny of accounts

Charities and other not-for-profit organisations must observe the statutory obligations that apply to them with regard to external scrutiny of their annual accounts (eg compulsory audit or, for some charities, the option of independent examination instead of audit). They may also have obligations arising from their own constitutions, which must be followed.

The precise statutory external scrutiny obligations for accounts vary according to the legal form of the organisation (eg a company) and any special legal status it has (such as charitable status). The charity law obligations also vary from one jurisdiction within the UK to another.

Statutory audit of a charity's annual accounts must be conducted by an independent individual who is a registered auditor (or an audit firm, with a named 'senior statutory auditor' taking overall responsibility for the audit). An audit involves obtaining evidence about the amounts and disclosures in the financial statements sufficient to give reasonable assurance that those financial statements are free from material misstatement, whether caused by fraud or error. This includes an assessment of whether the accounting policies are appropriate to the charitable company's circumstances and have been consistently applied and adequately disclosed; the reasonableness of significant accounting estimates made by the trustees; and the overall presentation of the financial statements.

The audit report is provided to the charity's members, if the charity is a membership charity (such as a charitable company limited by guarantee). It offers the auditor's opinion on whether the financial statements:

- give a true and fair view of the state of the charitable company's affairs as at 31 March 2011 and of its incoming resources and application of resources, including its income and expenditure, for the year then ended;

- have been properly prepared in accordance with UK Generally Accepted Accounting Practice; and

- have been prepared in accordance with the requirements of relevant legislation (eg the Companies Act 2006 for a charitable company).

Independent examination is a significantly different process to audit. An independent examiner does not scrutinise a charity's accounts to the same level as would be the case in an audit. The Charity Commission's directions for independent examiners will be followed (see CC32 *Independent Examination of Charity Accounts: Examiner's Guide*), so that the examiner follows a 12-stage process (or a six-step one under the relevant OSCR guidance, if the examiner is considering the accounts of a charity that is subject to the Scottish scrutiny regulations).

In England and Wales, the examination includes a review of the accounting records kept by the charity and a comparison of the accounts presented with those records. It also includes consideration of any unusual items or disclosures in the accounts, and the seeking of explanations from the trustees concerning any such matters. The procedures undertaken do not provide all the evidence that would be required in an audit and, consequently no opinion is given as to whether the accounts present a 'true and fair view'.

An independent examiner's report is given in connection with the examination. It offers a negative assurance that no matter has come to the examiner's attention:

- which gives the examiner reasonable cause to believe that, in any material respect, the requirements:

  - to keep accounting records in accordance with applicable legal requirements, and

> – to prepare accounts which accord with the accounting records and to comply with the accounting requirements of relevant legal requirements,
>
> have not been met; or

- to which, in the examiner's opinion, attention should be drawn in order to enable a proper understanding of the accounts to be reached.

Trustees should not over-rely on the end of year external scrutiny of a charity's accounts, which is no substitute for sound financial management, good internal controls and the proper discharge of the trustees' own responsibilities for the charity and its affairs.

For more information about the statutory external scrutiny obligations, see Chapter 5.

7.9   Health and safety

An organisation has general health and safety responsibilities in respect of its employees, its volunteers, visitors to its premises and, in some respects, to the general public. A charity is therefore required to take reasonable precautions to ensure safety at its premises and in its activities. There are additional specific statutory requirements in relation to the health and safety of employees (see para 7.9.1). Collectively, these legal obligations are wide ranging and should be taken seriously at all levels in the organisation. The charity's managers and trustees must give adequate attention to all matters of health and safety.

7.9.1   Health and safety of employees

Employers have a general responsibility to provide a safe place of work for their employees. Whilst safety from physical harm is a key aspect of this, the responsibility also extends to provide, so far as reasonably practicable, that employees are not harmed by activities such as harassment, bullying or discrimination.

A number of detailed specific statutory obligations also apply to employers, for example in relation to:

- manual handling;
- visual display equipment;
- fire awareness and fire safety training;

- first aid staff and services (this can include provision of facilities, equipment and training, the detail will depend on the nature of the activities and the levels of types of hazards involved);

- control of potentially hazardous substances;

- recording and notification of incidents and accidents.

Employees have a legal responsibility to take reasonable care with regard to the health and safety of both themselves and their colleagues.

The Health and Safety Executive provides a wide range of guidance and useful resources (see www.hse.gov.uk).

7.10 Insurance

Most organisations are subject to a number of compulsory insurance obligations due to the nature of their activities or the assets they hold and make use of, for instance:

- employers' liability insurance;

- vehicle insurance (especially in relation to liabilities to third parties);

- public liability insurance with regard to premises.

Charity trustees should ensure a charity has all necessary compulsory insurances in place and also decide what other optional insurance cover is appropriate for the prudent management of the charity and the proper safeguarding of its assets. It is important that trustees pay sufficient attention to financial systems and controls, as well as other forms of risk identification and management, and do not over-rely on the uncertain, and often partial, protection of insurance.

Appendix 1
Role Descriptions

1A   Specimen role description for chairman

Chairman of [*name of charity*]

Charity no

Role   To lead the charity's board of trustees, ensuring that it fulfils its responsibilities for the governance of the charity and to work in partnership with the chief executive, helping that chief executive to pursue the charity's charitable purposes effectively; and to optimise the relationship between the trustees, the staff and volunteers.

Responsibilities

- Leadership of the board of trustees (as the governing body of the charity) in its role of setting the direction and strategy of the charity.

- Ensuring that the board of trustees acts in furtherance of the charity's charitable purposes.

- Ensuring that the board of trustees deploys the charity's resources to further the charity's charitable purposes and in accordance with legal requirements.

- Planning the annual cycle of board meetings and committee meetings.

- Setting the agenda for meetings of the board of trustees.

- Monitoring that decisions taken at board meetings are implemented.

Duties

Examples

- Chairing meetings of the board of trustees and [*the Finance & General Purposes Committee*].

- Liaising regularly with the chief executive to maintain an overview of the charity's affairs and to provide support and guidance as appropriate.

- Representing the charity when appropriate at functions and meetings.

- Acting as a spokesperson when appropriate.

- Leading the process of appraising the chief executive.

- Sitting on appointment panels for senior staff.

- Chairing pay review group.

- Sitting on disciplinary panels.

Notes

1. This specimen is intended for use by a charity that has an employed chief executive and staff team. Appropriate adjustments should be made if using for a purely volunteer-run charity.

2. Adopt terminology as appropriate (eg 'chief executive' or 'chief executive officer', 'board of trustees' or 'council of management'). Ensure consistency with the charity's constitution, with staff job descriptions, etc.

1B Specimen role description for secretary of an unincorporated membership charity

Secretary of [*name of charity*]

Charity no

Role   To ensure that the conduct of the charity complies with all relevant requirements of charity law; and to support the chairman by ensuring the smooth functioning of the board of trustees.

Responsibilities

- Ensuring that relevant legal requirements are drawn to the attention of trustees and are complied with.

- Ensuring that proper arrangements are made for the calling, conduct and recording of annual meetings or other formal meetings of the charity's members.

- Ensuring that all matters relating to the admission and cessation of membership of the charity and the appointment or cessation of office of trustees and officers are conducted in accordance with the charity's constitution.

- Ensuring that proper arrangements are made for the calling, conduct and recording of trustees' meetings.

Duties

Examples

The following duties may be delegated to staff or volunteers in whole or part but it remains the responsibility of the secretary to ensure that they are carried out:

- Preparing documents for, ensuring the proper conduct of and making records of all formal meetings of the members.

- Preparing documents for, ensuring the proper conduct of and making records of all trustees' meetings.

- Ensuring necessary actions are taken in consequence of meetings.

- Ensuring required documents and information are provided to the Charity Commission and/or the Office of the Scottish Charity Regulator (as appropriate).

Note

1. This specimen can be adapted for a clerk to the trustees of an unincorporated charitable trust (delete references to members and members' meetings in that case).

1C   Specimen role description for secretary of a charitable company

Secretary of [*name of charity*]

Charity no

Role   To ensure that the conduct of the charity
                  complies with all relevant requirements of charity
                  and company law; and to support the chairman
                  by ensuring the smooth functioning of the board
                  of trustees.

Responsibilities

- Ensuring that relevant legal requirements are drawn to the attention of trustees and are complied with.

- Ensuring that proper arrangements are made for the calling, conduct and recording of the annual general meeting or other general meetings of the charity's members.

- Ensuring that all matters relating to the admission and cessation of membership of the charity and the appointment or cessation of office of trustees and officers are conducted in accordance with the charity's articles of association.

- Ensuring that proper arrangements are made for the calling, conduct and recording of trustees' meetings.

- Ensuring that statutory registers are kept as required by the Companies Act 2006 and associated regulations.

Duties

Examples

The following duties may be delegated to staff or volunteers in whole or part but it remains the responsibility of the secretary to ensure that they are carried out:

- Preparing documents for, ensuring the proper conduct of and making records of all general meetings of the members.

- Preparing documents for, ensuring the proper conduct of and making records of all trustees' meetings.

- Ensuring necessary actions are taken in consequence of meetings.

- Ensuring required documents and information are provided to the Registrar of Companies and the Charity Commission and/or the Office of the Scottish Charity Regulator (as appropriate).

- Ensuring the charity keeps statutory registers in compliance with the Companies Act 2006 and relevant regulations.

1D   Specimen role description for treasurer

Treasurer of [*name of charity*]

Charity no

Role	To maintain an overview of the charity's financial affairs, ensuring that it is financially viable, that proper financial procedures are operated and that proper records are kept.

Responsibilities

- Ensuring that the financial resources of the charity meet its present and future needs and obligations.

- Ensuring that the charity has and follows an appropriate policy on financial reserves.

- Ensuring that proper accounting records are kept.

- Ensuring that appropriate accounting procedures and controls are in place.

- Advising on the financial implications of the charity's [*5-year*] plan.

- Ensuring that the charity has and follows an appropriate investment policy.

- Ensuring that there is no conflict between any investment held and the charitable purposes of the charity.

- Ensuring that all legal restrictions on funds, investments and fundraising are complied with.

- Ensuring that the accounts are audited or independently examined in the manner in accordance with applicable accounting standards required by law (if applicable) and that any recommendations of the auditor or independent examiner are implemented.

- Ensuring that the accounts are prepared in the form required by law and the relevant regulations, in particular the Charity Commission and/or the Office of the Scottish Charity Regulator [*and the Registrar of Companies*].

Duties

Examples

- Overseeing, approving and presenting budgets, accounts and financial statements.

- Preparing and presenting (together with staff) financial reports to the trustees.

- Keeping trustees informed about their financial duties and responsibilities.

- Liaising with staff and volunteers as necessary concerning financial matters.

- Contributing to the setting of the fundraising strategy of the charity.

- Making a formal presentation of the accounts at the annual general meeting, drawing attention to important points in an accessible manner.*

- Sitting on the Finance & General Purposes Committee.

- Sitting on recruitment and disciplinary panels as required.

Notes

1.   If the charity is unincorporated it is not necessary for the annual accounts to be filed with Registrar of Companies.

*   Delete if the charity does not have a formal membership (eg it is an unincorporated charitable trust) or is not obliged to hold annual general meetings and present its annual accounts at such meetings.

1E   Specimen role description for charity trustee

Trustee of [*name of charity*]

Charity no

Role	To ensure, with the other trustees, that the charity acts in accordance with its constitution and to manage its activities in furtherance of the charitable purposes set out in that constitution.
Note	*The charity is registered a charity [and a limited company] [in the form of an unincorporated trust]. Every trustee [is also a director of the company and] has legal responsibilities and potential liabilities in [each] [that] capacity. Full details of these are not included in this role description but can be obtained from the charity's office.*

Responsibilities

- Setting the strategy and undertaking the strategic management of the charity.

- Ensuring that the charity complies with its [*articles of association*] [*trust deed*] [*constitution*] and all applicable legislation and regulations.

- Ensuring that the charity pursues charitable purposes as set out in its [*articles*] [*trust deed*] [*constitution*].

- Ensuring that the charity applies its resources in pursuance of its charitable purposes and provides appropriate public benefit through its activities in pursuit of those purposes.

- Ensuring the financial stability of the charity.

- Ensuring proper accounting records are kept.

- Ensuring the effective and efficient administration of the charity.

- Protecting and managing the property of the charity.

- Ensuring the proper investment of the charity's funds.

- Approving the charity's policies.
- Safeguarding the good name and ethos of the charity.

Duties

Collective

Examples

- Approving the rolling [*5-year*] plan annually and monitoring progress against it.
- Determining/approving the annual budget and monitoring progress against it.
- Preparing and approving the annual report and accounts.
- Appointing the chief executive and monitoring that person's performance.

Individual

Examples

- Attending meetings of trustees.
- Playing an active part in the trustees' meetings and deliberations.
- Exercising due care and attention and using reasonable skill in dealing with the charity's affairs.
- Using the trustee's own skills, knowledge and experience to help the board of trustees reach sound decisions.
- Taking the lead in any trustees' activities where the trustee has special knowledge.
- Avoiding any conflict of interests and declaring potential conflicts to the board of trustees.
- Sitting on the Finance & General Purposes Committee when required.
- Serving on one or more [*committees*] [*sub-committees*] [*advisory groups*].
- Sitting on recruitment and disciplinary panels if required.

Appendix 2
Model Declarations

2A Model declaration – candidate for charity trusteeship (unincorporated charity)

Name of charity

Charity no

Declaration

Full name

....

I, the undersigned, declare and confirm:

1. That I am willing to act as a trustee of the above charity ('the Charity').

2. That I will observe at all times all the requirements of the constitution of the Charity.

3. That I am aware of the Charity's charitable purposes (its objects) and will use my best endeavours to ensure the Charity pursues those purposes and operates in accordance with charity law requirements.

4. My company directorships of UK companies are (if none please state 'None'):

    _____

    _____

5. My other trusteeships of charities in England and Wales or Scotland or Northern Ireland are [*include full name and registered charity numbers(s)*] (if none please state 'None'):

    _____

    _____

6.   I do not have any financial or other personal interests which do or may conflict with the Charity's interests or charitable purposes either in person or by reason of my family, business interests or otherwise and I will notify the Charity should any such conflicting interests arise in future.

7.   I have the following interests in other organisations whose interests might at some time conflict with those of the Charity (please detail organisation and nature of the interest):

_____

_____

8.   I am aged 18 or over.

9.   I further declare that:

-    I am not disqualified from acting as a charity trustee.

-    I have not been convicted of an offence involving deception or dishonesty (or any such conviction is legally regarded as spent).

-    I have not been involved in tax fraud.

-    I am not an undischarged bankrupt.

-    I have not made compositions or arrangements with my creditors from which I have not been discharged.

-    I have not been removed from serving as a charity trustee, or been stopped from acting in a management position within a charity.

-    I have not been disqualified from serving as a company director.

-    I will at all times ensure the charity's funds, and charity tax reliefs received by this organisation, are used only for charitable purposes.

Signed ....

Date ....

Home address

....

....

Previous address if moved in past 12 months

....

....

Email address (it saves the Charity costs if we can contact you by email)

....

Date of birth

....

Please use this space to give any additional information you wish to supply:

Notes

1. This model addresses basic legal criteria for eligibility for charity trusteeship, as well as the 'fit and proper persons' test (for charity tax reliefs) and conflicts of interest issues.

2. Also check compliance with any additional eligibility criteria set out in the charity's own constitution (eg that candidates must be formal legal members of the charity).

2B   Model declaration – candidate for charity trusteeship (charitable company)

Name of charity

Charity no

Company no

Declaration

Full name

....

I, the undersigned, declare and confirm:

1.   That I am willing to act as a trustee of the above charity ('the Charity').

2.   That I will observe at all times all the requirements of the articles of association of the Charity.

3.   That I am aware of the Charity's charitable purposes (its objects) and will use my best endeavours to ensure the Charity pursues those purposes and operates in accordance with charity law requirements.

4.   My company directorships of UK companies are (if none please state 'None'):

_____

_____

_____

5.   My other trusteeships of charities in England and Wales or Scotland or Northern Ireland are [*include full name and registered charity numbers(s)*] (if none please state 'None'):

_____

_____

_____

6.   I do not have any financial or other personal interests which do or may conflict with the Charity's interests or charitable purposes either in person or by reason of my family, business interests or otherwise and I will notify the Charity should any such conflicting interests arise in future.

7.   I have the following interests in other organisations whose interests might at some time conflict with those of the Charity (please detail organisation and nature of the interest):

_____

_____

_____

8.   I am aged 16 or over.

9.   I further declare that:

  •   I am not disqualified from acting as a charity trustee.

  •   I have not been convicted of an offence involving deception or dishonesty (or any such conviction is legally regarded as spent).

  •   I have not been involved in tax fraud.

  •   I am not an undischarged bankrupt.

  •   I have not made compositions or arrangements with my creditors from which I have not been discharged.

  •   I have not been removed from serving as a charity trustee, or been stopped from acting in a management position within a charity.

  •   I have not been disqualified from serving as a company director.

  •   I will at all times ensure the charity's funds, and charity tax reliefs received by this organisation, are used only for charitable purposes.

Signed ....

Date ....

Home address

....

....

Previous address if moved in past 12 months

....

....

Email address (it saves the Charity costs if we can contact you by email)

....

Date of birth

....

Please use this space to give any additional information you wish to supply:

Notes

1.   This model addresses basic legal criteria for eligibility for charity trusteeship as well as the 'fit and proper persons' test (for charity tax reliefs) and conflicts of interest issues.

2.   Also check compliance with any additional eligibility criteria set out in the charity's articles of association (eg that candidates must be formal legal members of the charity).

3.   The statutory minimum age for company directorship is 16 (Companies Act 2006).

Appendix 3
Membership

3A Membership application form (charitable company)

Charity name

Company no

Charity no

To the Trustees of the above-named charity

[*Address*]

I hereby apply to become a member of the above-named charitable company and agree to guarantee the sum of [£1] in accordance with the articles of association of the company and company law.

I agree to be bound by and comply with the provisions of the articles of association of the company.

I am happy to receive communications from the company by email (including notices of general meetings, documents relating to such meetings and annual accounts and reports). This email address can be used for these purposes until further notice:

Email address: _____

Accordingly I authorise you to enter my name and other details in the register of members.

Signature: _____

Name: _____

Date: _____

Address to be recorded in the register of members:

_____

_____

_____

Postcode:

_____

Notes

1. Adjust guarantee sum if necessary (it is usually £1 but may be more).

2. Adjust as necessary if the company makes its annual accounts, etc available to members on a website.

3. Check that an applicant meets any eligibility criteria for membership specified by the articles.

4. The application may require formal approval by the board of trustees (check the articles).

5. The board should authorise registration of a new member in the register of members. The applicant becomes a legal member when the registration occurs.

3B Membership resignation (charitable company)

Charity name

Company no

Charity no

To the Trustees of the above-named charity

[*Address*]

I hereby resign as a member of the above-named charitable company with immediate effect.

Signature: _____

Name: _____

Date: _____

Address:

_____

_____

_____

Postcode: _____

Note

1. An appropriate entry should be made on the former member's entry in the register of members, to record the resignation. (Note the entry should not be entirely deleted.)

Appendix 4
Useful Contacts

Action Fraud

The UK's fraud information, advice and reporting service, operated by the National Fraud Authority

0300 123 2040

www.actionfraud.org.uk

action.fraud@nfa.gsi.gov.uk

To report suspected fraud, go to www.actionfraud.police.uk/report_fraud

Association of Chief Executives of Voluntary Organisations

1 New Oxford Street, London WC1A 1NU

020 7280 4960

www.acevo.org.uk

info@acevo.org.uk

Association of Chief Officers of Scottish Voluntary Organisations

Thorn House, 5 Rose Street, Edinburgh EH2 2PR

0131 243 2755

www.acosvo.org.uk

office@acosvo.org.uk

Bank Safe Online

The UK banking industry's initiative to help banking users stay safe online

www.banksafeonline.org.uk

advice@banksafeonline.org.uk

Burton Sweet

Pembroke House, 15 Pembroke Road, Clifton, Bristol BS8 3BA

0117 914 2057

www.burton-sweet.co.uk

charities@burton-sweet.co.uk

Charity Commission

0845 300 0218

www.charitycommission.gov.uk

enquiries@charitycommission.gov.uk

Charity Commission for Northern Ireland

028 3832 0220

www.charitycommissionni.org.uk

admin@charitycommissionni.org.uk

Charity Comms

The professional membership body for charity communicators

2–6 Tenter Ground, Spitalfields, London E1 7NH

020 7426 8877

www.charitycomms.org.uk

Charity Finance Directors' Group

CAN Mezzanine, 49–51 East Road, Old Street, London N1 6AH

0845 345 3192

www.cfdg.org.uk

Charity Law Association

01634 373253

www.charitylawassociation.org.uk

admin@charitylawassociation.org.uk

Charity Tax Group

Church House, Great Smith Street, London SW1P 3AZ

020 7222 1265

www.ctrg.org.uk

info@charitytax.info

Companies House

Crown Way, Maindy, Cardiff CF14 3UZ

4th Floor, Edinburgh Quay 2, 139 Fountainbridge, Edinburgh EH3 9FF

Second Floor, The Linenhall, 32–38 Linenhall Street, Belfast BT2 8BG

0303 1234 500

www.companieshouse.gov.uk

Fraud Advisory Panel

Chartered Accountants' Hall, PO Box 433, Moorgate Place, London EC2P 2BJ

020 7920 8721

www.fraudadvisorypanel.org

info@fraudadvisorypanel.org

Fundraising Standards Board

61 London Fruit Exchange, Brushfield Street, London E1 6EP

0845 402 5442

www.frsb.org.uk

info@frsb.org.uk

Get Safe Online

Expert advice from the Serious and Organised Crime Agency and other government bodies about how to be safe online

www.getsafeonline.org

Health & Safety Executive

Redgrave Court, Merton Road, Bootle, Merseyside L20 7HS

0151 951 4000

www.hse.gov.uk

HM Revenue & Customs Charities

St Johns House, Merton Road, Liverpool L75 1BB

0845 302 0203 (Charities Helpline)

www.hmrc.gov.uk/charities

Identity Theft

The UK's major investigatory and police authorities, including the Serious and Organised Crime Agency, the Metropolitan Police and the City of London Police, and other official agencies provide identity theft information and advice.

www.identitytheft.org.uk

Information Commissioner

Wycliffe House, Water Lane, Wilmslow, Cheshire SK9 5AF

0303 123 1113

www.ico.gov.uk

Institute of Fundraising

Park Place, 12 Lawn Lane, London SW8 1UD

020 7840 1000

www.institute-of-fundraising.org.uk

enquiries@institute-of-fundraising.org.uk

The Institute of Chartered Secretaries and Administrators

Charity Secretaries Group, 16 Park Crescent, London W1B 1AH

020 7580 4741

www.icsa.org.uk

info@icsaglobal.com

Institute of Legacy Management

2–6 Tenter Ground, London E1 7NH

020 7426 8875

www.legacymanagement.org.uk

rosie@legacymanagement.org.uk

Intellectual Property Office

Concept House, Cardiff Road, Newport NP10 8QQ

0300 300 2000

www.ipo.gov.uk

information@ipo.gov.uk

National Association for Voluntary and Community Action

The Tower, 2 Furnival Square, Sheffield S1 4QL

0114 278 6636

www.navca.org.uk

navca@navca.org.uk

National Council for Voluntary Organisations

Regent's Wharf, 8 All Saints Street, London N1 9RL

020 7713 6161

www.ncvo-vol.org.uk

ncvo@ncvo-vol.org.uk

Northern Ireland Council for Voluntary Action

61 Duncairn Gardens, Belfast BT15 2GB

028 9087 7777

www.nicva.org

info@nicva.org

The Office of the Scottish Charity Regulator

2nd Floor, Quadrant House, 9 Riverside Drive, Dundee DD1 4NY

01382 220446

www.oscr.org.uk

info@oscr.org.uk

Office for Civil Society

Part of the Cabinet Office

70 Whitehall, London SW1A 2AS

020 7276 3000

www.cabinetoffice.gov.uk/big-society

publiccorrespondence@cabinet-office.gsi.gov.uk

Regulator of Community Interest Companies

CIC Regulator, Room 3.68, Companies House, Crown Way, Cardiff CF14 3UZ

029 2034 6228 (24-hour voicemail service)

www.bis.gov.uk/cicregulator

cicregulator@companieshouse.gov.uk

Scottish Charity Finance Directors' Group

0141 560 4092

www.scfdg.org.uk

icameron@a-m-s-online.com

Scottish Council for Voluntary Organisations

Mansfield Traquair Centre, 15 Mansfield Place, Edinburgh EH3 6BB

0131 474 8000

www.scvo.org.uk

enquiries@scvo.org.uk

Small Charities Coalition/Charity Trustee Network

24 Stephenson Way, London NW1 2DP

020 7391 4812

www.smallcharities.org.uk

info@smallcharities.org.uk

Volunteer Development Scotland

Jubilee House, Forthside Way, Stirling FK8 1QZ

01786 479593

www.vds.org.uk

vds@vds.org.uk

Volunteering England

Regent's Wharf, 8 All Saints Street, London N1 9RL

020 7520 8900

www.volunteering.org.uk

volunteering@volunteering.org.uk

Volunteer Scotland

www.volunteerscotland.org.uk

Volunteering Wales

www.volunteering-wales.net

Wales Council for Voluntary Action

Baltic House, Mount Stuart Square, Cardiff Bay, Cardiff CF10 5FH

0800 2888 329

www.wcva.org.uk

enquiries@wcva.org.uk